MAY THIS TRUE STORY
CREATE A DEEP APPRECIATION
OF LIFE AND LIBERTY!

Mark Lee Myun

THE TOMATO SMUGGLER

How One Man Stood Up
to Communism

Mark Lee Myers

Published by Mark Myers Books
www.MarkMyersBooks.com

10 9 8 7 6 5 4 3 2 1
Front Cover Design by Guy Manzur, www.guymananimations.com
Typeset by Iryna Spica, spicabookdesign.com
The publisher is not responsible for websites (or their content) that are not owned by the publisher.

Published in the United States of America
ISBNs:
978-1-77374-064-5 (Paperback)
978-1-77374-065-2 (Hardcover)

"A remarkable, tensely exciting, moving true account. The energy of the narrative will stimulate any reader." —Dr. Mark Stock, former Assistant Professor, University of Wyoming

"A natural storyteller. Mark draws the reader into the storyline, exposing the forces of an oppressive regime that many in the free world have never known nor lived under its heavy hand. There is much to learn that will inspire readers currently at a crossroads politically." —Paul Lentz, author of "The Stuff of Life" trilogy

"I loved reading about the creative ways Nicolae's father coped with communist oppression. Mark Lee Myers does an excellent job of portraying life under a communist dictatorship, where many freedoms we take for granted are denied." —Sharon Marchisello, author of *Going Home* and *Secrets of the Galapagos*

To
Gabriela & Stefan

Table of Contents

Preface

I have been a child of privilege, though I did not think so before learning this story. While I was enjoying the comforts and pleasures of life in America as a young boy, a lad in Romania, Nicolae Cismigiu, was living under conditions of communism. For me, freedom was a given, but for him it was only a dream.

His was a country rich in beautiful people and places but ravaged by the occupation of foreign authorities and internal dictators. From the time of signing the 1944 armistice with the Soviet Union, communism had corrupted the fabric of Romanian society, unraveling thread by thread the dignity of life and transferring the power of privilege to those too calloused to care about the damage they were doing.

The socialist experiment did not work as advertised. Some of the communist ideals sounded good, but they failed when implemented by self-serving bureaucrats. They robbed the human spirit of any desire or motivation to excel. The Communist Manifesto was "from each according to their ability, to each according to their need." The Cismigiu family creed, unwritten but lived, was to work hard, persevere, prosper, and help others.

The terrorizing effects of communism had long been part of Romanian history. The 1917 Bolshevik Revolution in Russia is credited for also establishing Marxist communism in Romania. Nicolae remembers stories about his grandparents living through the 1920 bomb attacks orchestrated by partisan groups against the government.

Aside from cowards who benefited from human suffering and suppression, most Romanians did not want communism any more than the majority of the human race. But human behavior often is driven by survival instincts and fear.

It was mandatory after 1947 to join the Communist Party. Some people resisted by fleeing and hiding, but then were hunted down both outside and within Romania. Many people registered as Communist supporters merely to preserve their livelihood, with no heart for their actions. This was true even within the ranks of Communist authorities. There was some good among the bad. It was a dangerous balancing act where individuals in the government could have been severely punished for showing simple acts of kindness and leniency.

Political power struggles might have economic effect on the masses, but rarely are they designed to benefit the average citizen. Romania was no exception. The political elite led an extensive propaganda campaign to convince citizens that forfeiture of land and liberties would lead to more peace and propriety. But the communist ideals of Dictator Nicolae Ceaușescu (1967-1989) simply led Romania to the brink of starvation.

The Iron Curtain was both a physical and ideological barrier that separated the Soviet bloc from the West. Its veil obscured the view of truth from both sides. Those living behind its shroud, blanketed with communism, had little exposure to the Western life of liberty. Communist control stifled the flow of news in or out of the country.

The Tomato Smuggler brings to life the heart-wrenching reality of enduring harassment and intimidation in 1980s Communist Romania. The story satisfies curiosity about living behind the Iron Curtain and under the influence of communism during pre-internet Romania.

Tensions between Communist-controlled countries and those opposed to their aggression could be strongly felt during the tumultuous years between 1947 and 1991. In the 1980s, most of the world might have lived only with the fear of the Cold War; the Cismigiu family lived right in the shadow of its ugly influence.

The family built a thriving tomato business. Their tomato field was a symbol of their struggle for independence and freedom—their struggle for life. The local Communist authorities despised the father's ingenuity and success. There seemed to be hatred bred by jealousy, envy, and stupidity from Communist authorities too calloused to care about the damage they were doing.

The father led his family to both subtle and overt resistance. He was driven by an inner strength that influenced every aspect of the family life. The mother also paid both a monetary and emotional price to ensure her children were well educated and prepared for a better future.

I was introduced to Nicolae when I was forty-seven years old and he was thirty-eight. I sensed there was a depth to him from the moment we met during a job interview. Call it a sixth sense. Call it intuition. He was genuine. I felt a depth of maturity and character no textbook could have taught him. Our mutual respect encouraged Nicolae to share a very personal portion of his life's experience with me. The realism of the story captivated and inspired me. Everyone has a life story to tell, but the riveting reality of Nicolae's narrative has portions I wanted to preserve for their historical richness and others to prevent history from being able to repeat itself.

—Mark Lee Myers

Prologue

THE workhorse reared up, kicking with a vengeance. His owner, struggling to keep a firm grip on the neck rope, scrambled to avoid the horse's hooves. The stallion couldn't be tamed; his ill temper could kill a man.

The owner shouted. "This horse is a demon! He needs to be shot!" The man's struggle was interrupted by my father's booming voice.

"I'll buy the horse!"

~ Summer 2005 ~

Memories like this one race through my mind as I stand at the edge of what used to be my father's tomato field in Torceşti, Romania.

When the news of my father's death had come the year before, I was unprepared for the immense feeling of loss. There was nothing I could have done to prolong his life, nor would I have wanted to draw out his suffering. But I had missed attending the funeral with my family and the closure that would have accompanied it.

My father, Ionel Cismigiu, grew up in the small town of Umbrăreşti, Romania. No one remembers exactly why or when he acquired the nickname of "Cuţa" (pronounced "Coot-za"). My mother, Antonia, still lives here on our family farm.

My father was a large figure in my life, even though he only stood five foot, six inches. He carried himself like a gentleman, shoulders square, hair combed to the right or straight back, so he looked stately in an overcoat or blazer. He had a warm and confident personality, but he was also stern and determined. He was not afraid of anything, which his stocky physique personified.

The workhorse stallion, Simi, became a vital member of our family. In this regard, he was very much unlike the Communist Party. My father's reaction to and relationship with the stallion came to symbolize and emphasize his core character. I wonder if, like the horse, there might have been many Communist officials who came to quietly respect my father's fearlessness, seeing that he meant no harm.

Many Romanians under communist rule have a life story to tell. But our family's experience was unique due to choices my father made to protect us from communist oppression and the care our mother took to prepare us for a better life.

My father, scarred by the brutality he had witnessed as a child, vowed to never surrender to the Romanian Communists. He waged a war without bullets to retain our family's dignity and enraged the Communist-elite by often beating them at their own game. As a result, harassment and intimidation were a bitter concoction our family sometimes had to drink. We did not like the taste, but the alternative was to live in the shadow of oppression that stifled human spirit.

I am proud of my parents—very proud. Their lifelong zeal to keep the spirit of freedom alive came at a cost that many could not pay. Their determination was an inspiration, a beacon of hope to many weary Romanian hearts longing for liberty and darkened by the disillusion of communist ideals. Joy and sorrow were interwoven into the fabric of our family's life story, but we focused on happiness and contentment.

My grandpa always believed the Americans would come and liberate Romania after WWII. He never lived to see the day, but ironically, his dream did come true. It skipped a generation and impacted me.

It has been decades since I worked in this tomato field at the age of ten in 1981. It feels good to be back. It is time for this visit. I am ready for this reflection. There are stories my son has never known and several that even my wife has never heard. They are timeless stories that people in every generation, in every country, can identify with.

MARK LEE MYERS

Many people endure hardships and long for liberty, but many have no idea of the perseverance required to prevail.

My father's wisdom echoes in my ears. "Make your own destiny. Don't let anyone rob you of your dreams."

Stepping forward and bending down, I lift a handful of warm soil, sifting it through my fingers and trying to connect with the past. The smell reminds me of the bountiful harvest and the opposition we encountered to get it. My imagination holds the leathery scent of our workhorse and the earthy fragrance of the freshly plowed field. I brush the dust on my jeans as I straighten, inhaling the crisp morning air. I hold my breath and close my eyes, then release the air through pursed lips, reluctant to let it go. I open my eyes again, slowly scanning every detail. Something deep inside me rises to the surface, and my senses float into the past.

As I walk across the field, I feel the warm wind brush my face, bringing with it childhood memories. I look to see where it is going and drift with the wave of nostalgia.

1

Tortured

~ Fall 1981 ~

SCHOOL was in full swing, and I found it difficult to wake up on time during the week. Weekends normally allowed me to sleep in a little, but on this particular Saturday, I had asked Mom to wake me early. I loved helping Dad work outdoors. It excused me from household chores and thrust me outside and where I most wanted to be. I was more adventurous than my brother or sister, so I volunteered for great outdoor escapades.

I rushed through my morning routine to join Dad outside. He was inside one of the several tomato greenhouses that occupied our property.

This greenhouse, unlike the others, was ten yards wide and twenty yards long and stood only three to four feet off the ground. It had a chest-deep trench, dug out by hand, extending the full length through the middle, and on either side, the earth was dug down about a foot from the surrounding ground. The exposed wall of dirt acted as an insulator around the interior of the greenhouse and made a planting bed.

"Hi, Dad," I said, stooping down to enter the doorway. I climbed down the steps, and Dad smiled when he saw me.

"Good to see you up early," he said. "Working men don't sleep late."

"I would have been here sooner, but Mom made me eat breakfast."

"Good for her. Digging dirt in the woods requires lots of energy. We need fresh top soil to fill the planting beds." He pointed to the earthen shelves that extended out on each side of the trench. Dad knew where to find rich soil … free. Mother Nature had an endless supply for the taking in the rich bed under the canopy of forest trees.

We climbed out of the greenhouse and walked to the barn. Our workhorse, Mircea, heard us coming and let out a soft neigh.

"Grab a bucket of oats for him while I get his harness," Dad instructed.

I enjoyed feeding Mircea from a bucket. With his long nose marauding deep in the pail, I had little fear he would bite me. Up close, I inhaled his sandalwood scent.

With Mircea fed and hitched to the wagon, Dad climbed up to sit on the wagon seat, and I hopped into the wooden box formed by four outward-slanting side rails that outlined the wagon bed. I liked standing in the front of the box to look over Dad's shoulder as I rode along. The side rails were designed to either sit atop our wagon or homemade sled. We used the sled when snow covered the ground. The wooden box easily held two cubic yards of dirt.

Dad nudged Mircea forward with a verbal click and flick of the reins. I stood tall with a smile on my face. We didn't exchange much conversation, but instead, we listened to the whistle of the wind and the hoof-beat of the horse.

When we got to the woods, Mircea wove through the canopy of trees at his master's signal. Dad studied the variety of trees as much as the forest floor. Sunbeams filtered through the tree canopy, illuminating a patchwork quilt design on the rusty-colored autumn leaves. When Dad found the spot he was searching for, I grabbed my small shovel and helped him clear the area to expose the dirt. Shoveling was hard work, but it gave me a sense of pride to be included, even if I wasn't much help because I soon tired.

After several minutes, I planted my shovel in the dirt and leaned on the handle.

MARK LEE MYERS

"Are you tired already?" Dad asked me. He flung a spade of dirt over his shoulder into the wagon box.

My arms and upper back burned, but rather than admit it, I redirected the conversation.

"Will we ever run out of soil for the greenhouses?"

Dad chuckled. "I doubt it. God has given us more than enough good soil. I can't wait to show you some of the most beautiful and expansive forests next year when we travel to market through the Carpathians."

I was looking forward to that adventure. When I was younger, I would have simply been in the way. I straightened my shoulders and stood a bit taller.

"Why do the Communists always try to stop us from growing and selling our tomatoes?" I asked.

"Our family's struggle with the Communists began before President Ceaușescu took office and way before you were born, Son," Dad answered. "It started with your grandfather. He died the same year you were born, which is why we named you after him. He was a great man who stood firm in his convictions about freedom and fairness. Grandma Maria died less than two months before Grandpa Neculai did. Grandma was the heartbeat of his life. When she died, so did his will to live."

"What did the Communists do to Grandpa?" I asked.

"Well, I was ten years old when a very traumatic thing happened, and since you're ten now, I think you're mature enough to learn a significant part of the story." Dad stuck his shovel in the dirt and motioned for me to sit next to him on a fallen log.

~ Summer 1946 ~

THE police roared into the driveway, spewing pebbles into the yard and dust into the air. They had come many times before to harass and intimidate, so their arrival was no surprise. What was surprising, however, was the attitude of their approach on this particular occasion. Vehicle doors flew open before the wheels came to a complete stop, and men jumped out with malicious expressions. Before a word was spoken, it was apparent they were on a serious mission.

"Mr. Cismigiu!" one shouted in an authoritative voice. "Come outside immediately, or we will forcefully enter."

Several officers had exited the far side of their vehicles and remained there. They had heard that Neculai had a stash of hunting rifles, and they kept the vehicles between themselves and the farmhouse windows. The air was stagnant and heavy. The disturbed dust rolled away from the vehicles like waves in slow motion.

Neculai Cismigiu exited the front door as stately as his name sounded. His wife, Maria, and his son watched anxiously from the window. His expression was not of surprise or alarm, nor was it threatening. He simply locked eyes on the lieutenant and kept walking forward off the porch. He knew who had yelled his name.

The other officers stood on full alert, their body language directing attention to the lieutenant. Not a word was spoken. The crunch of gravel pierced the silence as Neculai walked across the driveway. He stopped and faced the lieutenant, close enough for a handshake that did not happen.

Lieutenant Victor Căpreanu was a familiar face and name to Neculai. The police force and officials assigned to govern a city, county, or region were made up predominately of citizens from the same area. Others might be transferred in from the outside to ensure proper training and adherence to the communist rules, but often one's new worst enemy might have been an old acquaintance. Lieutenant Victor and Neculai had been schoolmates and had known each other since youth. They were never close friends in school, but they had not been enemies either.

The lieutenant exhibited a billy goat nature, not content until he had bullied his way to the top. It did not matter if anything or anyone got knocked off in the process. He had often drawn attention to himself by force.

Victor and Neculai had chosen vastly different paths in life. Victor had embraced communist ideals once he realized that such a pursuit was a fast track to the top of a rocky pinnacle. Communism needed a heavy hand to enforce infringement of liberty. This suited Victor's personality.

The established elite in Bucharest may not have approved of all his methods, but at certain times, they probably found a ruthless man like Victor useful. This was one of those moments.

"Hello, Victor."

The eyes of Victor's posse darted between the faces of the two men. Neculai was unarmed, but one officer cautiously moved his right arm backward, resting a palm on his holstered revolver. Tension filled the air.

Neculai spoke calmly. "You called me out here ... and here I am."

"You have lied to us," Lieutenant Căpreanu accused. "I will ask you once more, and only once, to surrender your guns. We have more than one witness who provided all the proof we need that you have guns. We are not going to waste any more time looking for them. You, Mr. Cismigiu, will tell us where they are immediately. If you don't, you will wish you had."

Neculai suspected that neighbors, hoping to gain personal favor, had become informants and told the authorities that he was harboring undisclosed firearms.

"I can't give you," he stressed, "what I don't have."

He knew exactly where the guns were hidden. He had wrapped them in protective cloth and lowered them into an abandoned well. But it was true that he did not have them at the moment. The guns were safely out of reach.

Victor lunged forward and swung his right fist upward and jabbed deeply into Neculai's gut. Victor's arm was massive and his punch powerful.

Neculai had no time to tighten his abdomen to absorb the blow. The shock wave shot upward through his chest cavity, forcing the air from his lungs and bruising many organs along its path. Neculai doubled over. Stones punctured his knees as his body sank to the ground.

Victor kicked his foot outward, catching Neculai in the crotch then smashed his knee into Neculai's face as he fell forward.

———

Watching from the window, Maria gasped. She grabbed Cuța by the arm as he darted for the front door.

"Son, I know how you feel," she said, and then lowered her voice. "If only I had one of his guns! I would aim for the heart of the savage."

———

Neculai curled onto his side and vomited.

Victor was not finished. He grabbed Neculai's hair, yanking his head back at an odd angle.

"Have I made myself clear?" he roared.

Neculai did not answer. Victor released his hold with a thrust, and dust and gravel scattered when Neculai's head bounced off the ground.

Victor circled his prey.

Neculai gasped for air as he rolled to his knees and tried to stand. Blood dripped from Neculai's mouth. He braced his hands on his thighs, pushed himself to an upright position, and turned to face his opponent.

"I didn't hear your answer," Victor sneered.

Neculai whispered distinctly. "You ... will ... never ... get ... my ... guns."

"Ah, so now you admit you have them," Victor said triumphantly. He snapped his fingers and an officer appeared at his side.

"Prepare the boiling water," Victor ordered.

Officer Gheorghe sprinted to the porch. Neculai flinched, as if to give chase, then grabbed his bruised rib cage.

"Don't worry, Neculai." Victor laughed. "We are not here to torture your wife. That might be another day, if you don't cooperate. We're simply going to borrow a little water and boil it on your stove." Victor's voice thickened with sarcasm. "Your wife won't object, will she?"

The house door crashed open as Officer Gheorghe bolted through it. Maria screamed. She grabbed Cuţa's hand, and the two ran to the bedroom and shoved the door shut.

Cupboard doors slammed and pans clanged as the officer searched for a large stove pot. Moments later, water could be heard sloshing from a bucket to fill the chosen vessel.

Victor retrieved a pack of cigarettes, sliding it slowly from his shirt pocket. He ran his finger over the cigarette filters, as if counting, and then pinched the last one, extracting and lifting it to his lips with the theatrics of a man with whom time was of no concern. Lighting it, Victor inhaled deeply ... and then aimed and blew a dense cloud of smoke into Neculai's face.

Neculai dodged and stumbled.

"I strongly advise you to stay right here," Victor said. "Don't even think about leaving."

Neculai glared at the Lieutenant and Victor smirked. This was not a time for words.

———

Officer Gheorghe came out of the house carrying the steaming pot of boiling water. Lieutenant Victor motioned to another officer on the opposite side of a nearby police vehicle. The officer reached inside and grabbed something off the floorboard. As he rounded the rear of the vehicle, in the officer's hands were polished knee-high military boots.

Neculai's eyes widened.

A wicked grin curled the edge of Victor's lips as he took the boots. He placed them carefully on the ground in front of each of Neculai's feet with precision, as if to avoid marring the polish. He stepped back and with a nod beckoned Officer Gheorghe to pour the boiling water into each boot.

"Don't make the mistake of disobeying me again, Mr. Cismigiu."

Maybe there is a twinge of guilt hidden deep within the man after all, Neculai thought. Maybe Victor can't use my first name, as that is too personal for what he is about to demand.

"Step into the boots and shove your feet to the bottoms," Victor commanded. "Do *not* test my patience, or I'll drag your wife out here and give you the privilege of watching her do the honors."

Neculai closed his eyes and drew in a long, deep breath. He would never allow a finger of Victor to touch and harm his wife, but to willfully step into boots of boiling water was an action beyond courage.

Victor and Gheorghe grabbed Neculai, and he stiffened but did not struggle. Hoisting his bruised body, the two men hovered Neculai over the boots, and Victor snarled. "Point your toes!"

———

Maria's face was buried in her bed pillow, one arm wrapped tightly around her son, her body trembling with tears. Her husband's scream pierced the air but did not drown out the roar of laughter from Lieutenant Victor.

Vehicle doors slammed and tires spun as the officers sped away.

Maria ran through the house and out the front door. Her son could outrun his mother in a normal footrace, but this was nothing normal. She was jumping off the front porch when her son sprang from the front door.

Neculai had collapsed on the ground and fainted from the pain. Steaming water poured from the boots and soaked into the dry ground. Maria knelt at his side, caressing his head and screaming for help.

Cuța stood frozen with shock at the sight of his father's raw, red legs. He did not know what to do. To pull off the boots would rip the flesh away. The scalding water had already emptied. He approached his mom and stood behind her, reaching down to hug her shoulders as she rocked and sobbed.

"Run, Cuța," she whimpered, her voice trembling. "Run for help!"

———

Dad and I sat in silence for a moment. I didn't know what to say or do. There was a faraway look in his eyes. He finally turned toward me.

"That moment changed me forever, Son," he said, shaking his head. "Since that day, I've had a hatred for communism. Just like your grandfather, I knew I could never surrender my pride and sign my allegiance to that party and its ideals."

"Did they ever torture Grandpa again?" I asked.

"They tortured him repeatedly, and not just physically. The Communists took land, guns, and freedom from many families. Grandfather lost a lot of land, but he never revealed his hidden stash of guns. He loved to hunt."

Hunting was a dream for me. "Will we ever be able to go hunting?"

"Sadly, we are not permitted to hunt anymore. The privilege only is granted to Communist Party members loyal to Dictator Ceaușescu. You, might share his first name, but that is the only thing I hope you ever have in common with him. As you know, I help Vasile, when the elites from Bucharest come to hunt after we get our first good snow."

I knew Vasile was the game warden in our county in addition to being the forest warden.

"Maybe I can ask permission for you to get close to the action," Dad said. "It might be easier to obtain Vasile's permission than your mother's." Dad smiled and laid a hand on my shoulder. "Let's finish filling this wagon before lunch."

He stood, grabbed his shovel, and continued tossing soil into the box. I rose slowly from the log, my mind reeling with the story he'd told me, trying to imagine what stepping into a boot filled with boiling water would feel like. As I shoveled, I thought wistfully about the grandfather I had never met.

———

When we returned home, we unloaded the soil onto a large pile near the greenhouses. After lunch, we shoveled the dirt from the pile into a suspended wooden frame where a wire mesh separated the small rocks, roots, and sticks.

We mixed the clean soil with the right amount of sand and aged chicken and cow manure to create the perfect consistency. This was our secret recipe.

2

Simi

~ Fall 1981 ~

SHOUTS of men and the sound of chainsaws surrounded me as I sat on the seat of my father's horse-drawn wagon. Many local homeowners in rural Romania depended on firewood harvested from these forest trees to heat their houses. The late autumn air was crisp and invigorating with the sun's rays strong enough to warm the forest floor.

"What's the price for one this size?" a customer asked above the noise. The forest warden measured the circumference of the tree, stepped back, and estimated the height. He quoted the man a price, payable to the government coffers, and the customer agreed.

The warden then approached my father, who was sizing up a tree nearby.

"Good morning, Vasile," Dad said. "It's a great day for cutting firewood."

"It is," Vasile agreed, shaking Dad's hand. Vasile looked up at me on the wagon and smiled.

"Are you here to watch or to work?" Vasile teased. I grinned. Vasile knew a ten-year-old wouldn't be much help cutting firewood, but he knew I loved being with my father in the woods.

Vasile looked official in his government-supplied uniform: khaki green trousers and jacket. He was older than my father, and maybe an inch or two taller, which made him look thinner. His hair was brown with streaks of gray, and if he had a government-issued hat, he never wore it, so his hair was always wind-blown and uncombed. I only saw him in his warden-at-work capacity, so I remember him as rugged.

The government owned the vast acres of timber and assigned wardens in each county to regulate firewood harvesting. The forest warden was responsible for deciding which trees were suitable for harvesting and then painting white bands around their trunks. Vasile was a Communist loyalist, but only on paper. He was a rugged Romanian at heart, doing his best to survive and provide an honest living for his family.

Dad and Vasile had developed a great friendship, as they were the same age and shared a love for the forest green and its serenity. Vasile appreciated my father volunteering for such tasks as marking trees for harvesting and anything that required more than two strong arms and one strong back.

As a forest warden, Vasile didn't have to worry much about his Communist superiors' watchful eyes. He was trusted as a government loyalist and gained a sense of autonomy by performing his duties. Because of my father's prestige for growing tomatoes, Vasile had solicited his training to learn gardening skills. The two partnered to grow tomatoes on a plot of government land Vasile managed. They split the work and profits. The Communist officials never found out about it.

"Where's Simi today?" Dad asked, referring to Vasile's temperamental stallion.

Vasile pointed through the trees. "I tied him up over there away from the others," he said. "He's in quite the mood today. Honestly, I have a hard time controlling him, and I'm afraid someday he'll hurt someone."

My eyes followed where Vasile pointed. I saw Simi in the distance tied to a tree, pawing the ground and tugging the reins.

Simi was not an average horse. Most large-bodied workhorses are, by nature, gentle and easy to work with. But Simi had a contrary nature. No one knew Simi's true bloodline, but Dad suspected he was part Ardennes crossbred by the Germans during their occupation of Romania in the early 1940s.

Simi's coat was shiny and chocolate brown, rippled with layers of muscle that appeared flexed even when relaxed. His massive body was supported by solid black legs and large hooves with slightly feathered fetlocks. His neck was as thick as an oak and was decorated by a black mane. His broad hindquarters were flagged with a black tail. Not a rib was evident, unlike so many other horses in our region. His large head and dark, piercing eyes gave him a formidable look.

Dad often spoke of Simi after returning from a day helping Vasile. He was in awe of the horse's magnificent physique and amazed by the confidence with which the stallion approached strenuous tasks.

We heard a commotion to our left and turned to see several men attempting to push a wagon laden with logs out of the mud. Two horses strained against their harnesses as the driver whipped the reins in a futile effort to free the wagon.

"That looks like a job for Simi," Dad said, raising his eyebrows and flipping his thumb in the direction of the ruckus. "Would you mind me using Simi to help them pull the wagon free?"

Vasile shrugged. "Do what you want. I've got other customers to help." Then he looked at me, furrowed his brow, and warned, "Don't turn your back on him. He'll grab you by his teeth and throw you off balance."

Dad tied our horse to a tree. I jumped down from the wagon seat and followed Dad as he made his way through the trees toward Simi.

When Dad got close, Simi turned to face him and pinned his ears back in aggression. Dad didn't even flinch; he lunged toward the horse so boldly that Simi scuttled backward. Dad was not afraid, and the stallion knew it.

Having established his dominance, Dad untied the horse and led him toward the stuck wagon. As we neared the commotion, Simi began to trot, forcing us to jog beside him. Simi had obviously been through this routine before and seemed anxious to show off his strength to the observers—both horses and men.

By the time we reached the wagon, the men had given up, exasperated. All eyes turned to Dad and Simi.

"Unhitch both your horses," Dad instructed the driver.

The man furrowed his brow. "Do you really think you can pull the wagon out with only one horse?"

"Trust me, he's done it many times," Dad replied. The man hesitated for a moment, then stepped down, unhitched his horses, and led them off to one side.

Dad maneuvered Simi into position and strapped the strong leather breeching strap to the wagon shaft and hooked the trace chains to the harness hame tugs. He held the reins and stepped slightly to the side in front of the horse.

On Dad's cue, Simi leaned his weight against the harness, straining forward. I had seen most horses in this situation bolt and either break the chains or feel the weight against their harness and back off. But Simi instinctively knew better. His hooves stomped and scrambled to get traction in the muck, splattering mud in all directions. He slipped, falling to his knees, his nose dipping into the puddle on the ground. He even tried to crawl forward in this crouched position to maintain his forward motion. The horse's eyes widened and nostrils flared.

Simi did not know when to stop and could easily overexert. "Easy boy," Dad said, grabbing hold of Simi's bridle as the horse rose to stand once again.

Dad knew how to manage Simi's zealousness. The stallion seemed to sense that Dad was not asking him to give up; Dad was letting him rest before exerting again. Simi's body language communicated that quitting was not an option.

"Okay, let's try again." Dad didn't need to coax. Simi was ready.

The wagon creaked and its wheels made a sucking sound as Simi found firm footing and steadily pulled the load free from the mire.

The men stood in silent awe, coveting the beast and its beauty. Leading his two horses, the owner approached, incredulous. Dad unhitched Simi from the wagon.

"That was very impressive," he said. "Tell Vasile I said 'thank you.'"

Dad nodded, but before he could say anything, Simi lunged and nipped one of the other horses. Snorting in anger, Simi and the horse began to scuffle, and the other horse bolted, ripping the reins from the owner's hands. As the fight escalated and the horses whirled in circles, men yelled commands that did little to calm the situation.

Having heard all the ruckus, Vasile came running.

"Does anyone have a rope?" he shouted.

The owner grabbed one from under his wagon seat and tossed it to Vasile. Vasile improvised a lasso and flung it around Simi's neck to pull him away from the fight. He would have been held responsible if Simi injured or killed the other horse.

The stallion reared up and kicked at Vasile. "Whoa!" he shouted. Vasile stumbled as the weight of the horse jerked the rope backward, and he dodged to avoid the horse's hooves.

Vasile twisted his head to glance at my father, his wide eyes begging for help. "This horse is a demon! He needs to be shot!"

Dad's booming voice interrupted the commotion. "I'll buy the horse!"

Dad grabbed the rope from Vasile and yanked it downward, grasping Simi's bridle with the other hand. Simi snorted in indignation but immediately submitted.

"He's all yours," Vasile said, shaking his head and looking relieved.

———

The sounds of chainsaws finally faded at dusk. Weary men gathered the small limbs scattered around the forest floor. Nothing was wasted. Dad often used small limbs to build a slow burning fire for distilling *pálinka*—a homemade plum brandy.

Tomorrow, the gypsies would clean up anything that we missed. They would find more than they expected. I saw Dad purposely leave some firewood and small limbs behind for them to glean.

Vasile agreed to trade Simi for Dad's horse, despite the fact it wasn't quite a fair trade. Simi could do twice the work. I think the forest warden knew that when Dad came back to lend a helping hand, he would bring Simi, and Vasile would benefit without being responsible for the cantankerous horse.

The ride home was as long and the wagon as heavy as it had ever been, but to me, it felt like we were floating. Simi pulled the wagon effortlessly, his large hooves creating a clip-clop that echoed through the night. As we approached our farm gate, I jumped down and swung it open before running toward the house.

"Come out and see what we got today!" I shouted to alert anyone inside. I leapt onto the front porch and turned to watch Dad drive Simi into the yard. I didn't know much about horses, but there was something special about Simi beyond simple equine anatomy.

I felt a strong sense that Simi would become a vital part of our family.

3

More Land Than Allowed

~ Summer 1963 ~

ROMANIAN farmland is rich and fertile. High humus content makes it arable and perfect for pasturage, vineyards, and orchards. Because the land is one of the country's most valuable resources, the Communist government officials attempted to confiscate and limit its ownership. Driven by greed and control, they deprived owners of their assets and forced them to labor for the system.

One government strategy was the systematic takeover of the countryside. This scheme destroyed villages and resettled residents into agro-industrial communes. The government fooled Romanian citizens into thinking they could work for the government and enjoy urban life while having all their needs met. "Needs" were defined by the government. This was ruthless power and pillage on a grand scale, otherwise.

Anyone who owned too much land was considered an enemy of the state. If a farmer dared acquire more than one-quarter of an acre, either the government would tax excessively or dictate what must be grown on it. In rural areas where farming practices were the mainstay, the communist government softened the blow of confiscation by offering farmers a small percentage of the crop harvest profits. The weight of intimidation was too great for the broken and fragile spirits of many Romanians ravaged by years of World War II occupation and now communist corruption. Those who succumbed to this "bargain" were often forced to work for the government on their own land.

Entrepreneurship runs in the blood of my ancestors like water flows in the river. Communism dammed the river but couldn't stop the water from rising and spilling over. The inner fortitude of my grandparents and great-grandparents was remarkable. My great-grandpa on my father's side had owned an inn and restaurant at the crossroads in Umbrăreşti.

Umbrăreşti lies peacefully in the Siret River Valley, about thirty miles from the eastern Romanian border and slightly south of mid-center. The Siret River snakes a few miles to the west, and flat, fertile farmland stretches in all directions.

The inn was famous for its food. Romanian meals were seldom without cabbage rolls, called *sarmale,* and the recipe served at Great-Grandpa's inn was so delicious it could have passed for the main course. The wonderful aroma enticed many a weary traveler to go the extra mile—or ten—to reach the inn by nightfall.

My father's parents were well known in the Siret River Valley in the historical region of Moldova. They had accumulated more than one hundred acres of land through years of toil and tenacity. My grandparents never signed communist loyalty papers, but even if they had, the government would still have seized their land, animals, and property. Practically everything except for their home and the small parcel of land it was built on was stolen by the government. My grandparents also lost ownership of their inn and restaurant. Communists hated entrepreneurs, especially those who were not members of the party.

Because the government had confiscated the parcel of land my grandparents intended for my father and his new bride, Father spent his savings to purchase land about three miles from the homestead in the town of Torceşti. Life experience taught him to think ahead and to hope for the best but plan for the worst, so my father approached the church and purchased the tract of land from a priest. Church-owned property was immune from government control and confiscation, so Father hoped the land would remain protected, but a corrupt government can uphold or annul any law or contract at any time without the will of the people. Not surprisingly, my parents later discovered the ruling Communist Party abided by a different law and repeatedly tried to lay claim to their property.

The land Father purchased in 1963 for his new family's home was more land than was allowed. The property had more road-frontage than most, which offered another potential target. A common tactic of land confiscation was for a claim of excessive land—excessive as defined by Communist bureaucrats—to be subdivided, leaving only the home and a little bit of land around it.

Father attempted to make his property less desirable for subdividing by designing a long, single-story home and a barn. Both were situated parallel to the road-frontage to cover as much width as possible.

Father knew he needed to begin construction with haste because the longer the newly acquired land sat empty, the greater chance the authorities would discover his purchase and devise a strategy to confiscate it. The government could also limit access to building supplies, thereby controlling area construction. The clock was ticking.

Father, ever the entrepreneur, never missed a golden opportunity to make or save money. He heard from friends that there was an abundance of construction wood in the northern mountains.

Father inquired and found a man who was willing to sell a huge, commercial-sized wooden barn. The wood was aged but of great quality, so my father hired men to disassemble the barn, stack it on a flatbed semitrailer, and transport it from the mountains to Torceşti.

There was so much lumber from the disassembled barn that only half was used to build the new home and small barn. Father sold the other half to men in the community for more money than it had cost him.

It was a modest home, not because of lack of money but because my parents tried not to draw attention. The home included three bedrooms, a small living room, a kitchen, and a bathroom.

Our parents established their life together for four years before being blessed with a family of their own. In 1967, my brother, Marin, was born, and two years later came my sister, Lenuța. I was born two years after that in 1971.

I was destined to be different. My siblings' blue eyes matched Dad's, but the blue-brown gene combination of my parents' eyes colored mine green. My siblings even favored Dad's build in height and strong, square shoulders. I always seemed to be the skinny one. But I also turned out to be the tallest in my family.

A single woodstove heated our home inadequately, so we didn't use some of the rooms in the winter. My brother and I shared a bedroom off the living area, and we left the door open to allow the heat to radiate inside. We never let our four-year age difference create a conflict with our shared room. Bedrooms were for sleeping, and we were usually sufficiently tired at bedtime. My sister slept in our parents' bedroom because her bedroom was located too far away from the woodstove. Sharing the confined space undoubtedly contributed to the closeness our family enjoyed.

In the field behind our home, my father planted his first tomato plants—the product that became our means of survival. Not only was my father a farmer at heart, but frankly, he had no other option. He was never offered a good government job after refusing to sign communist loyalty documents. My father loved his little farm. He could sense the soil fertility by rubbing it gently through his fingers and inhaling its earthy aroma. He respected and cared for it, and in return, the land always provided a wonderful harvest. "Give and you shall receive," was his motto.

Communism tried to create a new society and a new man. Father was already the man he desired to be. He certainly did not need any help from the government. He vowed that no Communist would ever take his farm. He had paid for it. He had cared for it. He would keep it.

No one knew the hardship that decision would bring to our family.

MARK LEE MYERS

4

Take My Hand

~ Winter 1981 ~

SNOWFLAKES fell like cotton and clung to every surface. I had a love-hate relationship with wintertime. I loved playing in the snow with my friends, and I hated that I had to sacrifice playtime to help prepare for spring on the farm.

Temperatures dipped colder than usual, forcing us indoors where there was plenty of work to do. We huddled around a woodstove, rolling six- by twelve-inch plastic sheets into cylinders and stapling them to form tomato transplant containers.

Prior to springtime, we would snuggly pack each plastic sheath with soil and poke a hole into the middle for inserting the tomato-plant seedling when it had sprouted six-inches high. Into some, we directly planted tomato seeds. We would then cluster the containers on the floor of another greenhouse.

We made thousands of these each winter. To pass the time, we begged Mom and Dad to tell us stories. At twelve, my sister, Lenuţa, was beginning to notice boys. She was the most interested in romance stories.

"Where did Dad take you on your first date, Mom?" Lenuţa asked. This wasn't a question I would've asked, but anything to break up the monotony of manufacturing cone cups was a welcome distraction.

I held the plastic cylinder I had been rolling and lifted my eyes to look at Mom. She had an air of authority I respected but also the kindness of a loving mother. I had seen photographs of her with longer hair when she was younger, but now her thick hair was cut short and rounded out her facial features. Mom met Dad's blue-eyed gaze and smiled, as if exchanging thoughts with him we couldn't hear.

"Your father was quite the romantic," she chuckled. I glanced at Dad and saw him blush ever so slightly. Mom sat back in her chair, her hands resting on her lap, deep in thought. I could tell she was remembering another time and place we knew nothing about. "I knew from the time we started dating that I wanted to marry your father. We did a lot of fun things together and loved the time we courted."

~ Summer 1962 ~

THERE were two forms of entertainment for teenagers in the '60s in rural parts of Romania: weddings and county fairs. Both were essential to the courtship of Cuța and Antonia.

County fairs in the Moldova region of Romania were not a one-time annual event, nor a carnival, as might be the custom in rural parts of other countries. The purpose of the fairs was to get young people together on weekends during the summer and fall. The local Communist authorities did not organize the events but permitted them as long as they didn't develop any anti-government undertones.

The county fairs mainly revolved around food and music, more like a barn dance.

The aroma of cooking sausage and the drumbeat of country music permeated the air. The tempo and volume of music was as much to draw attendance as it was to debut musical talent. Gypsies often were enlisted to play and sing. Not all gypsies were nomads. The government provided plots of land for them to live on, so gypsies in our region were an active part of our lives.

The fairs were held on an open field outside of town and were always well attended. It was a place to be and be seen. Status was measured by having a good-looking horse and wagon.

These weekend wagons were not rustic cargo wagons but rather ornate open carriages with brass accents. Young men spent more time grooming their horses in preparation for a weekend excursion than finishing schoolwork. After all, what good was an education without status and a beautiful lady sitting beside them on their wagon seat?

Cuța was usually the designated driver of his father's passenger wagon for any weekend excursion with his friends and any female acquaintances they might pick up en route.

Trotting to the fairgrounds in luxury and style, Cuța did not yet own Simi, but he always had a great-looking breed. It was as much his horse as it was his wagon that turned people's heads and brought a smile of respect to their faces.

Antonia was a beautiful girl with wavy, dark brown, almost black hair, flowing just below her shoulders, a full figure, and a look of innocence and confidence. She had no shortage of suitors, but she hated to be obligated to dance the entire evening with any one young man who might buy her ticket to the county fair. She enjoyed her freedom, so she usually preferred to attend with her brothers. Young men begged her brothers to influence her interest, but the brothers were quite protective of their sister, so only a few suitors ever received the honor.

Cuța, however, secured a winning ticket. He stood out from the crowd, not because of his physical height but because of his character and charm. He knew Antonia's brothers well. They romped together. He had won the brothers' trust, and in turn, Antonia respected and admired Cuța. He told Antonia that she was not obligated to remain by his side all evening, although she gladly did.

Cuța and Antonia's friendship took root immediately. Cuța had planted a seed of courtship and nurtured the growth for maximum results. He attended to what made Antonia happy, and in return, she enjoyed spending most available weekends with him. It did not matter at all that Cuța was eight years older than Antonia's twenty years of age.

Antonia lived four miles away outside of Salcia, the next town. The miles passed quickly when Cuţa drove his horse and wagon to pick her up, but the distance seemed longer when he returned home alone after their dates.

———

Attending a weekend wedding was the second form of entertainment during their courtship. Romanian weddings are social events for the whole community.

The rigors of life in rural farming communities put a demand on the labor force from springtime to fall. Almost everyone was part of this labor force. This limited the window of opportunity to late September and October for courting couples to marry. In addition, an abundance of wine was desirable for a wedding, so if there was not enough remaining from the previous year, the wedding was postponed until the end of grape harvest in October.

The ceremony was private, but the wedding reception and festivities were public. Everyone in the community was invited. Scheduling was very important if the bride and groom wanted to have guests help celebrate. It was not uncommon for there to be three or four weddings on the same day. Couples tried to at least schedule staggered start times. Otherwise, they might have no attendees.

A huge, dark-gray vinyl tent was erected at the church in the town square, or if the groom's family property had enough room, the tent was put in their yard. Tables were set up inside the tent for the guests in three or four long rows. The wedding entourage sat at a separate, perpendicular table across one end. Handmade rugs with intricate woven patterns hung as a backdrop.

Many weekends, Cuţa picked up Antonia in his horse-drawn limousine, and the two of them hopped from one wedding to another. What better entertainment, especially for a dating couple, than to have free food and drinks almost every fall weekend?

So it was on a stunning afternoon conducive to romance in 1962 that the handsome Cuţa picked up Antonia for their usual wedding reception extravaganza. There were three weddings that autumn day—a full agenda—but instead of turning toward the town center, he steered the wagon toward the woods.

Antonia cocked her head and raised an eyebrow. With a faint smile, she looked at the handsome man holding the reins. He turned his head to catch her eye and winked.

Cuţa slapped the reins and his horse quickened the trot to a canter. They rode in silence, enjoying the warm breeze and rhythmic clatter of the horse's hooves. Antonia loved the thrill of wagon rides and outdoor adventure. She loved being with Cuţa. Out of the corner of her eye, she admired his rugged complexion and strong hands as he deftly handled the horse and wagon.

Cuţa navigated to a trail in the woods that sliced through a beautiful stand of timber near the Bârlad River. The smell of nature changed from the sweetened scent of countryside pasture to the earthy scent of leaves and tree bark. He slowed the horse to a trot and then to a walk. Nothing broke the stillness except the wind tickling the treetops and horse hooves scattering the leaves.

Cuţa leaned toward her and whispered, "I have a special place I want to take you."

"If it is special to you, then I'd love to go," Antonia answered.

He reined in the horse, and the wagon gently rocked to a halt. Cuţa jumped down and extended his hand to steady Antonia as she stepped from the wagon. When her feet touched the forest floor, he did not release her hand but interlocked their fingers and led her through the trees.

"Have you ever seen a Linden tree?" he asked.

"I know what one is, but I have not studied one up close," she replied.

"It is one of my favorites. I love what it symbolizes. It stands both majestic and romantic, with heart-shaped leaves. We will have to come back and see one in the springtime when it is covered with beautiful flowers."

The one right in front of them was a beautiful specimen. Antonia reached out and touched the tree bark with the palm of her free hand. Cuţa lifted her other hand and twirled her body with the graceful move of a ballroom dance to lean her against the tree trunk. He plucked a green leaf and held it at eye level between their gaze, twirling the heart shape between his thumb and first two fingers.

His smile broadened. "I don't have much to offer, but what I have I want to share with you: my hopes, my dreams, my life."

A tear formed at the corner of Antonia's eye, swelling until it rolled down her cheek. He caught it on the heart-shaped leaf. "I'll go anywhere with you," she whispered. "Sharing life with you will double my joy."

Their kiss was as gentle as the breeze, and their embrace as strong as the Linden, which would come to symbolize their enduring love.

———

Our parents were married the year after the romantic marriage proposal, in 1963. It was the only wedding on that day, so nearly everyone in town stopped by the reception to wish the newlyweds a wonderful life.

Dad's statement about not having much was true. By the time he married Mom, his parents had been forced to forfeit all of their vast property to the Communists, except for the small piece of land where their home was built. Our grandparents had been robbed of the Romanian tradition of sharing a portion of the family property with their children in the form of a starter home. Dad purposed to build his bride a home, a nice but modest home, with timber from the mountains. What Dad purposed, Dad did.

Perseverance would be our family's strength and bond. Life would be full of adversity, but life would be rich with experience. We would be taught that life is not what others make it to be, but what we make it to be.

5

Hunted

~ Winter 1981 ~

A PROMISE made is one I don't forget, so I begged my father to allow me to accompany him on the frontline action when the snow fell and the hunters came. He had been correct, Mom was not in favor, knowing there was more danger than the explosion of gunpowder. But persistence and pestering paid off.

"Wake up, Nicolae," Dad whispered, shaking my bed while trying not to rouse Marin. It was four a.m. I had not slept much. I had awakened on the hour, every hour, after Dad had agreed to take me to the woods.

We ate a quick breakfast, then went to the barn and harnessed Simi to the wooden sled box. Dad stepped on the front of the sled, braced himself, and held the reins as I jumped inside the box and stood behind him, leaning against the wooden frame. The temperature felt brisk as Simi trotted along, but my excitement was on fire.

Vasile asked my father to help during this hunting event each year. Vasile had heard stories about my father prior to being assigned his forest warden duties in Galați County, but the man who became his trusted friend was nothing like the one described by the regional authorities. Vasile enjoyed my father's camaraderie while helping with forestry duties throughout the year, having similar interests to discuss in the solitude of the woods. He trusted my father. As game warden, he also needed his help to satisfy the Communist elites from

Bucharest who came each winter to hunt in the woods near our home. More than Vasile's career was on the line.

Vasile respected my father's courage to withstand the harassment and intimidation from the Communist authorities. But he didn't want to put my father in a precarious position by having him work so up-close-and-personal with the elite bureaucrats who might know too much about our family legacy. Vasile spoke candidly about the dangers. "If the wrong official recognizes you, you might become the hunted," Vasile warned.

"I'm not afraid to defend myself if questioned, but I won't initiate the conversation. I'll concentrate on keeping the hunting party focused on the right prey," Dad said.

Vasile and his family lived right in the woods in a large home provided by the government. The lavish living accommodations provided to him were not based on his rank. The Communists were not generous by nature. The real reason was for maintaining a hunting lodge for the privileged few. The Communist elite had their own best interests at heart. Assigning a game warden, especially to areas of great hunting habitat, was to ensure top-quality game as a benefit for the Communist Party loyalists in the top tiers of President Ceauşescu's regime. The game warden was more a glorified servant whose real purpose was to entertain his hunting guests.

Vasile's wildlife management duties were significant and time consuming. The game warden was responsible for protecting wildlife from poachers, recording wildlife numbers and quality, and depositing food sources, including hay and alfalfa, at feeding stations set up at strategic locations within the vast woodlands. He welcomed my father's extra set of hands and eyes to tackle this huge undertaking. Wild boar, deer, and jackrabbits were the favored and plentiful game in our region of the Siret River Valley.

The arrival of Bucharest aristocrats in Galaţi County during hunting season signaled the start of a well-orchestrated hunting spectacle that engulfed many from the community. The Bucharest entourage arrived the afternoon prior to the first morning hunt and stayed at the lodge in the woods. The group was primarily Romanian government officials and an occasional visiting foreign dignitary, mostly European.

Citizens from the surrounding towns helped with cooking for days ahead and prepared for the comfort of the guests—everything from immaculate house cleaning to elaborate decorations fit for the occasion and honored dignitaries. Young and older men from the neighboring towns were grouped at specific times during each hunting day to walk through the woods in predetermined patterns and locations to drive the wild game. This channeled the game to the hunters perched on oversized, elevated platforms with comforts rarely afforded in the wilderness.

The hunting stands were shielded with walls on all four sides to protect the occupant from the chill of winter wind. A chest-high opening circled the platform and created a shooting window in all directions. A food box, occupying one side near the door, was stocked with cold-cut sandwiches and drinking water.

Dad's sled was a great help with transporting hay bales to food plots, hunters to hilltops, and carcasses to the butchering barn. Dad mingled with the visiting hierarchy, transporting them via horse-drawn sled to their hunting stands. They may have been accustomed to limousine rides to and from state dinners and official engagements, but no one seemed to mind the contrast of comforts provided by my father's transport service. In this rugged wilderness, the soft hay my father piled in the sled box was a cozy, rustic element that provided needed warmth and aesthetics.

"Welcome, Cuţa." Vasile smiled, as Simi pulled our sled up to the front of the hunting lodge. Our frosted breaths, including Simi's, rose and dissolved into the cold, windless air.

"A great day to hunt." Dad beamed.

"You brought a helper with you." Vasile looked at me with approval reflected in his raised eyebrow.

"The love of hunting runs in his blood," Dad said with a prideful grin.

Dad stepped off the sled and heartily shook Vasile's gloved hand. I had little expectation of what Dad would actually do with me today. I did not want to be in the way, but I wanted to be as close to the action and observant as possible. It caught me by surprise when Vasile directed his next question to me.

"Would you like to sit in a hunter's shooting box this morning?"

I was speechless … but I wanted to yell, "Yes!" I'm not sure if any audible response actually came out or not, but Vasile knew my answer. It was written all over my face.

The Communist official he assigned me to be with didn't seem to mind at all. I did not get to hold the gun or pull the trigger, but I felt connected with nature at a primitive level.

It was a magical moment climbing to the top of the hunting platform and sitting in silence before daybreak. The calm of darkness magnified my senses. The rhythm of my breathing and pulsating heartbeat became focal points.

Remembering that morning is as vivid as it was at that impressionable age of ten. I have relived it many times over and can now even better articulate the intensity of emotions I experienced. When the first hint of sunrays rang the horizon's doorbell, the cacophonous chorus of nature's orchestra started warming up. Then a momentary hush settled over the audience of forest inhabitants as, with anticipation, the curtain lifted. The majestic sun entered center stage like a charismatic maestro, and the stillness was once again pierced as the sounding stanza of wildlife and the wind in the treetops heralded the dawn of the new day.

Sunrays filtered through silhouetted trees, casting shadows across the landscape. I heard a soft rustling as the horde of scouts began their approach to drive the wildlife toward the hunters. As they neared, the sound intensified with the crunching of the crusted snow under their boots. Animals raced through the trees to escape the approaching intruders.

Snow blanketed the ground and clung to tree branches. The contrast of white magnified my depth perception by negating the natural forest camouflage, allowing the rampage of game to be seen long before it bounded into the clearing of shooting lanes. The volley of rifle shots cracked like steel whips. Some were close, piercing with ricocheting blasts, and some farther away, echoing with muted concussions.

Surprisingly, the hunters observed a custom of respect, waiting to field-dress the harvested game back in the sanctity of the hunting lodge barn by first covering the animals with oak leaves while bellowing traditional hunting tunes. Many of them might have been bad people, but they were good and respectful hunters.

Animal entrails had many culinary uses, and those that didn't were respectfully buried under the forest floor. They cleaned the carcasses and hung them for transport to Bucharest in refrigerated trucks.

Vasile discreetly culled out several selections of liver and heart for us to take home, assuring that the hunters would forget how many animals they had killed and never notice. We welcomed the gift. It added to our limited meat supply for the year.

The Communists killed many things. Life, liberty, and the pursuit of happiness were among the greatest casualties.

———

The area's citizens varied in their views of the yearly hunting season. Those in favor were farmers who routinely experienced crop damage from wildlife. The Communists did little about reported crop damage and loss of farmer income, but thankfully, their militant hunting escapades helped control wildlife population and provided a balance that inadvertently accomplished the relief farmers had petitioned for.

Those who were apathetic to the hunting spectacle had lost their emotions years earlier. It was routine to be summoned to participate in orchestrated group rallies of support for government propositions. Local residents might be asked to stand in town at the center square or along the streets holding pre-made signs that reflected positive statements on topics of interest to some visiting politician or for a film crew capturing the sentiment of the citizens for some newscast in a distant city or foreign broadcast. But it was seldom a true reflection, because rarely did the will of the governed agree with the will of the government: it was manufactured news, manufactured sentiment.

Hunting season was a very special time to me. Gunshots might have sounded oppressive to most people, but they had a liberating ring to me and worked a nostalgic magic. I dreamt of being like Grandpa, a rugged outdoorsman in tune with nature and at liberty to hunt.

6

Green Thumb

~ Spring 1982 ~

I REMEMBER Dad often saying, "If you can't feed yourself, you can't be free." That is why Dad loved gardening.

Winters were usually hard and springs late to arrive, and the threat of late frost kept farmers from sleeping well. It was a battle nature waged. Dad needed greenhouses to combat this enemy and win this war.

Our family's preparation of the greenhouses began in late January. Repairs often were needed, as the support structure was made from small trees or good-size limbs, flexible enough to be arched as beams over the top. We then covered the greenhouses with thick, transparent plastic to allow the natural sunlight in.

After the soil warmed, we started the seeding process. It amazed me how many tomato seeds Dad could palm at once—the dexterity with which he then rolled individual seeds between his thumb and index finger, simultaneously dispensing from both hands onto the soil in symmetrical rows. His movement was robotic as he stitched out two rows of seeds at a time. It was easy and fun for me to follow him and poke the seeds into the soft soil beds.

The plastic cylinder cups were more difficult to handle. We filled each with the secret soil mix, packed the dirt down a little, and buried a tomato seed below the surface. We stacked these cylinder cups upright against each other in row after row inside a second greenhouse. A week later, we planted a second generation of seeds into more cups. These extra cups were our backup plan to counter the Communists' harassment that would surely come, as it did nearly every spring.

A wood furnace located inside, with a chimney pipe running full length, heated each greenhouse when the temperature dropped below freezing. Dad would not delegate to anyone else the task of stoking these fires but coddled with care the temperature regulation inside the greenhouses. He packed wood chips and sawdust tightly into the stoves so the fire smoldered and burned with a nice even glow. Too much heat would kill the tender plants.

During harsh winters and late spring snows, Dad set his alarm clock and woke every two hours to feed the fires and brush the snow off the greenhouse roofs to prevent their collapse.

In the humidity, the rich soil and tomato plants produced a pungent smell. It was not unpleasant; to the farmer, it was the sweet smell of money.

When the tomato plants had grown at least six inches tall, we transplanted them to adjacent greenhouses and spaced them for sturdier and taller growth. In one greenhouse, Dad built long wooden boxes from two- by ten-inch lumber and filled them with his secret recipe soil mixture. One by one, we painstakingly transplanted thousands of plants from their starter home into rows six inches apart.

I hated this part of the job, but I remember Dad emphasizing, "This is not a hobby but a livelihood." Failure might mean starvation.

Dad designed a way to prevent the soil from being compacted while the six-inch-tall plants were being transplanted into the prepared soil boxes. He laid a simple sheet of plywood across the top edges of the wooden planter box, allowing a lightweight person to kneel on top while bending over to put the plants in the soil. We slid the plywood back as row after row of tomato plants were rooted in the soil. As the youngest and lightest, I was the prime candidate for this job, forced to kneel, hunched over, for hours at a time.

Dad also created another experimental greenhouse that was heated from decomposition. All the straw and manure cleaned from the horse barn was gathered in two or three compost piles outside. Each large pile became quite warm as it decomposed. He snuggled a wooden box frame into the top of each compost pile and filled a few inches short of the top with the planting soil. We covered the tomato seeds we planted inside these boxes with framed glass panels overlaid with the transparent plastic. The heat generated from the compost was perfect to initiate growth.

Dad learned the art of organic gardening from my grandpa, but he had never heard it called that. The style of farming we now know as "organic" was the commonsense way it had been done for centuries, maybe since the beginning of creation.

7

Springtime Start

~ Spring 1982 ~

I AWOKE to breakfast aromas wafting into my bedroom. I sprung out of bed and pulled on a pair of pants and a shirt before I ran through the kitchen, headed for the back door.

"Wait just a moment, young man." Mom grabbed my shirt sleeve. "You need to eat something if you're to be outdoors all day."

Springtime had arrived, as in most parts of the world, with singing birds, warm breezes, and blooming flowers. Today, I was anxious to help Dad plow the tomato field. My parents permitted me to stay home from school. I was a good student and loved learning, but I looked forward to this day every spring.

I plopped down at the table and Mom placed a plate in front of me. I ate, not because I was hungry, but because I could not waste time arguing.

I inhaled my food and then allowed Mom to plant a kiss on the top of my head before I flew out the back door and ran to the barn. Dad saw me coming and waved. When I ran up to him, he grabbed me in a headlock.

"Hey, Son," he greeted me, ruffling my hair with his fingers. Next to him, Dad's prized stallion, Simi, nickered a hello.

"Are you ready?" Dad asked.

"I was born ready," I replied. "At least, that's what Mom says. Something about me fighting like a tiger the day I was born."

He chuckled. "I remember—you roared like a lion."

I raised my shoulders and puffed out my chest.

"Now, let's see how much you remember from last year." He turned toward Simi. "I have his harness collar on. You show me what should be done next."

I ran my palm over the horse's coat, which was freshly brushed. I never saw other farmers brush their horses until the workday was finished.

I loved the care my father had for Simi; theirs was a relationship unlike any I knew.

Normally, a loving and lasting relationship begins with the ceremonial words *To have and to hold, for better or worse, till death do us part.* Simi was not my father's wife, but those words accurately described the commitment they shared.

Dad respected and needed Simi. The Communists did not permit us to own more than one horse, so we were fortunate in that Simi could do the work of two.

We were also not permitted to own a motorized vehicle, neither car nor tractor. All vehicles were truly a luxury, with greater demand than supply, so there was a waiting list. Dad's name was on the list, but it was no surprise that it never rose to the top. In our small town, few families had the money to buy a vehicle, but my father had the money for a brand new anything. However, the local Communist authorities curtailed his big-ticket purchases, hoping to make it more difficult for our family to thrive.

"I'll take the bridle, Dad." I knew he was warming it in his hands as he always did on crisp mornings—another act of kindness. The horse bowed his head and opened his mouth without a spoken command as I lifted the bridle and fit the bit as gently as I had always seen my father do.

I felt comfortable around Simi even though many were afraid of his ill temper. I respected his strength, and in turn, he respected me as his master's son.

I tightened the noseband, making sure to leave a two-finger width below the prominent cheekbone, and then fitted the throatlatch loose enough that two or three fingers could fit between it and Simi's neck.

Moving from the front to the rear of the stallion, I kept my hand in contact with his coat, then placed the harness breeching to the horse's hindquarters. I lifted his tail to slide the crupper under it and buckle it in place, and I made sure that the crupper was smooth and clean and that no hair was trapped under it.

I fastened the bellyband to the traces, which helped hold the harness in place. Then I checked the tension of the girth. It was important to ensure that the harness would not slip and strangle the animal if the plow was caught in action.

Once finished, I looked up at Dad and said, "I'll help you carry the plow." Dad could have carried it over by himself, but he waited for me to pick up the other side. A subtle smile teased the corners of his mouth; he knew I was delighted to help him do the simple tasks he could've completed by himself in less time.

Dad chose the first day in May to start planting the tomato field each year.

"I love the irony," Dad said. "This day is a communist holiday to celebrate the working class."

The intent was to have a day off to feast with family and friends, but Dad found it easier to hire help. Also, by this time, the seeds we had poked into our secret recipe soil in February had matured to impressive plants, strong enough to withstand the outside elements.

But farmers' fears were numerous, and Dad could not rest easy knowing there were forces beyond his control. Wind, rain, and hail were dreaded until harvest was completed, but the annual tomato war that loomed on the horizon was a far worse storm than any natural disaster. Dad braced for and feared it most.

Springtime meant new life, but what did the future hold? No guarantees, that was for sure! Even though I was young, I had maturity beyond my years. I remember my father saying, "I long for my children to live in freedom and liberty without the shadow of communist ideals stifling their human spirit."

These lessons were part of everyday life and engraved discipline and determination on my young heart. It would have been easy to become calloused by the weathering winds of opposition and oppression, but instead, my father showed by example how to live as an optimistic survivor. The innocence of my youth helped, but the influence of genetics and guidance from my father were shaping my personality. I could not have learned from a better man. My father was a determined hard-worker, a legend and true symbol of freedom.

8

Harassment & Intimidation

~ Spring 1982 ~

DAD was expecting them. Friends had learned of a surprise attack by local authorities on my father's tomato field and exposed the plan. There was little mention of the illegality of the raid or concern for any lack of humanitarian aspect in its execution. The advanced warning allowed Dad to uncap the water well and run the pump all night long to flood the tomato field.

I remember the gentle movements of my father's fingers placing a tender plant in the fertile soil. Just as vivid are the memories of ruthless, selfish men, trying to break the will of my father by destroying his crop at the start of almost every planting season.

Many families experienced hardships, but we endured additional difficulties due to our father's resistance. We had broken communist law and were harassed mercilessly for owning what the authorities considered too much land. The government had confiscated our excess property, at least on paper, yet we continued to plant tomato crops on that property each year, for which we were assessed a penalty we would never pay.

The government dictated what crop should be grown each year. Bureaucrats with little to no field experience made decisions not based on science but self-serving interests. The government hated competition, so they monopolized production through legislative dictatorship. They were empowered by ignorance and bred mediocrity.

It was not simply a monetary fine or imprisonment the authorities wanted from my father. They wanted to harass and intimidate him to a point of surrender—a surrender of land, a surrender of pride. These acts were justified in the eyes of the perpetrators because an example must be made of his defiance of government policies.

The attack came near daybreak.

The police approached my father for permission to enter on our property through the main gate. He obviously refused, and a skirmish ensued. Dad was a short and stocky man. He had been a formidable wrestler in his teenage years, and his years of hard work providing for his family and for many hungry fellow citizens had both strengthened his muscles and deepened his resolve. Few could get past him.

After Dad denied the police brigade entrance, they went to the neighbor on the back side and asked permission to enter the Cismigiu farm from his property. The neighbor agreed and took down a fence on the property line so the police could gain access to our farm.

Dad grabbed a pitchfork from the barn and ran to sit on the fence line where the attack commenced. He sat there and dared them to run him over.

He had bought a camera, and from the time I was five years old, he tasked me with taking pictures during the skirmishes. As I snapped the photographs of the battlefield, I felt the rush of adrenaline. I was scared.

The police always tried to provoke Dad to do something stupid. But he stood his ground. Often, the police tried to push him out of the way, hoping he would strike one of them. On this occasion, the police dragged my dad out of the way while he still was clutching the pitchfork. Dad never stabbed any of them with it—if he had, they would have taken him to jail.

Once they had access to the field, the police pretended to plow, but they actually only drove their tractors around at random to crush the tender tomato plants. They destroyed property just for the sake of it.

In the dim predawn light on this morning, when the police attempted to plow up the field and wreak havoc on the crops, we got the last laugh.

The tractors-turned-war machines became stuck in Dad's muddy fields. Shouts of frustration from the invading parties could be heard over the roar of tractor engines and spinning tires. At first, there was a barrage of blame hurled at each other, and then cries and commands for help from their comrades. The police used one tractor to pull the other out, which made a bigger mess.

Sadly, the influence of communism caused ordinary people to do terrible things. Many of the people who wore the uniform of authority lived in the same or nearby towns. These were not warring strangers—they knew each other!

A few of the invading entourage looked innocent dressed in their street clothes, but I learned quickly and early that looks are deceiving. The ringleader was often a particular lady—a non-elected city official—whose malice and meanness were disguised under her headscarf. She needed no uniform or badge of authority. We assumed she either received the commission to lead these bands of thugs because her demented disposition aligned so well with the desired pain wished upon our family, or that no one dared deny her demand. When and why her hatred for our family had begun was a mystery. It could have been jealousy.

The mayor was on hand as well; he was the son of my father's schoolmate, but today he was aligned with the police and the headscarfed honcho, or at least, not willing to oppose them. Dad crossed the field to where the mayor stood alone with his hands held behind his back and shoulders hunched, looking forlorn.

"Whose side are you on?"

The mayor was speechless and looked away. He rocked on the balls of his feet, as if he wanted to go somewhere, anywhere but here.

When the soldiers of destruction finished their mission, Dad confronted the headscarfed ringleader. "Are you pleased now?"

The answer was not verbal. She stomped her foot on a tender plant, grinding it into the dirt as if it was a cigarette butt.

The tomato field was not the only thing the Communists destroyed.

Dad's gardening skills were not only evidenced by his cultivation techniques using a special soil recipe or the quality and abundance of his tomato harvest. He also landscaped our farm with beautiful fruit trees and grape vines. An orchard of apple, cherry, and plum trees lined a fence, separating our property from a neighbor. He had purchased and propagated these varieties for their high yield and natural resistance to pests and disease. He mastered pruning, too.

Dad loved the art of pruning for both an esthetically pleasing appearance and maximizing production yields. Everyone has a different eye and sees life from a slightly different angle, so no two pruned trees look alike, especially when pruned by different people. Somehow, Dad's orchard was more beautiful than most.

The secret to pruning is hiding the cuts so that when done, especially after a few days of natural weathering from sun and rain, the plant looks as if it naturally grew that particular way. Dad wanted to step back and be pleased with the finished look, and if he accidentally cut too much, he knew that pruning was forgiving. With life, there is new growth, so every year he got new opportunities.

Where did he learn these techniques? In school? From a book? No. Nature was his best teacher. He knew that gravity works and always will, so he removed the lower branches to keep fruit from touching the ground. He also respected the tiers of a plant by giving every branch space to grow in unfiltered light without interference. If only the repressive government regimes of the world could understand and appreciate as much in relation to life, liberty, and the pursuit of happiness and fulfillment.

Unfortunately, the Romanian Communist dictatorship had bred an envious mentality that trickled down through its hierarchy into local municipalities. The Cismigiu farm was raided and my father's orchard trees were cut to the ground.

The shock of seeing them do it paralyzed me, but Dad sprung for the door.

Mom's voice got his attention. "It's not worth it!"

Dad paused, the door half opened.

Mom continued. "It's as futile as trying to prevent the tractors from trampling the tomato plants."

A moment of silence passed inside our home, and then the whack of wood as a tree limb plummeted to the ground outside.

Dad spoke, slowly shaking his head. "We're not dealing with rational behavior."

I wondered if he might have said this to convince himself and find meaning for the madness. He exhaled heavily, and his shoulders slightly sagged. And then, Dad deliberately inhaled slow and deep, forcing oxygen to swell his chest and lift his shoulders. *We will persevere.* The words were not audible, but they were the theme of our family's existence.

———

My father persisted. He was not easily uprooted. If they could not break the will of this tomato farmer, then they would turn their efforts of harassment and intimidation on his wife and children. The Cismigiu family must pay the price.

There was no retaliation or retribution possible. The judicial process was as corrupt as the Ceaușescu secret police. Dad often advanced his complaints before a local judge, even with stacks of photographs, but his pleas fell on the man's deaf ears and hardened heart.

We steadfastly endured our family burdens. There were two opponents in this brutal game—our family and the Communists. The system could beat us, or we could try to beat the system. If we gave in, we lost. If we withstood, we won—or at least retained our dignity.

9

Second Chance

~ Spring 1982 ~

I HOPED in my heart what I had witnessed and photographed the previous day had been a bad dream, but looking out my bedroom window this morning there was scattered carnage. Tomato plants lay trampled and water trenches were crushed in the zigzagged tractor tire tracks. I turned away and walked to the back door of our home, hesitating at the threshold.

This time, Dad decided to replant without delay. The replenishment plants in the greenhouse had grown almost taller than the plastic casings of dirt could support. If we did not transplant soon, we would be at risk of losing our second chance.

The sun was rising over the horizon behind the tomato field, casting a shadow from the distant trees over the landscape as I looked out the door. The mountain of effort awaiting us in the war-torn field looked higher and harder to climb from my young vantage point. We dreaded the destruction of the tomato crop each year. One might think our family would be inured to the ordeal given that it was expected, but expectation never took away the sting of devastation.

I am not sure if I felt more panic or pain. Our family depended upon a tomato cash crop, so there was no other option than to plant again. A second planting was a second chance, and harder work than the first.

Long before I came into the world, my father had envisioned what it would take to make his field uniquely different to allow high-end production of a tomato harvest. It began with the soil. He believed the soil should work for him rather than him struggling with it. I was not there to see the original years of laborious effort to construct the tomato field, but I remember hearing him explain how he did it.

"The first secret of success is proper irrigation," Dad said. "Tomato plants basking in the heat of the Siret River Valley sun are thirstier than a camel crossing the desert." I had never been to the desert or seen a camel crossing one, but I understood the analogy. A camel might have water on reserve, but the tender tomato plants required frequent replenishment.

He had taken the time to explain because he saw my interest. "To make the irrigation work, the field must slope from the front side nearest the water well to the far side near the back of our property." He added with a smile, "But neither the Creator nor the prior property owner had prepared the ground to my specifications."

Premeditated and calculated movements are required to level out mounds and fill in depressions in the landscape, especially when the goal is a gradual slope from one end of the field to the other. I am amazed at Dad's precision, considering he did not own modern and motorized farm machinery. He did not have use of a surveyor's transit, theodolite, or level. My father created his soil canvas on which he artfully grew his masterpiece tomatoes using the simple stroke of a horse and plow.

In the early years, Dad owned a horse, but it was not Simi, and from what Dad explained, he spent as much time steering that horse as he did manhandling the plow. I can hear Dad's hearty laugh when he spoke of the difference in the way Simi worked. He joked that he could attach the plow to Simi and give him one slap of the rein, and then sit back on the porch sipping lemonade while Simi worked on autopilot.

The field layout reminded me of an American football field with a trench furrowed down the center from one end to the other. Every ten yards there was a trench intersecting the middle one, extending out to the edge of the field on either side, so between each ten-yard line was essentially a rectangular box to the left and right of center. Within these rectangles there were many parallel trenches equally spaced out to the sidelines. Each furrow was carved out from a twin-blade plow to form irrigation trenches and mounded planting rows.

Dad understood that water always takes the path of least resistance and used that principle to his advantage when irrigating the tomato field. A second well behind our home was used for nonpotable indoor plumbing as well as irrigation. This water was pumped into a holding tank, and gravity pulled it into the house for inside use. For irrigation, the water was pumped directly from the well and directed to the center trough, which sloped down the middle of the tomato field. With a little persuasion, we diverted the water flow into each trough between the rows of tomato plants.

Before winter, after each harvesting season, Dad plowed the foliage into the soil, turning the ground as a baker folds flour into a lump of dough. He liked to expose the soil to the weathering of winter snows and spring rains to help decompose the plant material into revitalizing nutrients and to soften the earth. Each spring, therefore, the elaborate proportional design of interconnecting watering troughs was recreated by Dad with his horse and plow.

The police changed their tactics over time to combat my father's tenacity. The local authorities were as lazy as they were mean-spirited, so in the early years, they simply made a few circles crisscrossing through the tomato field on their tractors. As our family refused to be intimidated into submission, their show of force became stronger and their efforts to destroy property more damaging.

In the aftermath of the raid, where tyrants on tractors had slaughtered both tomato plants and irrigation trenches, we had to start over and redo all that we had painstakingly accomplished weeks or days prior. Each year, my father felt encouraged to dare a second planting only because the police had never destroyed the crop twice in one spring. But with communist behavior, one could expect the unexpected.

––––––

With the exception of Dad, we all worked basically the same amount of time, from morning to night. Dad stayed up late the night before reseeding began and rode a bicycle over seven miles round trip to enlist support from our gypsy friends. He also woke up before daybreak to make last-minute preparations for the planting party.

I felt my well of strength had dried up. This was work I had previously completed, and now it had to be done again.

I sat in the doorway, reluctant to leave, feeling half committed. I stared at the destruction in the field, which seemed to stretch to the horizon. I knew this work was vital to my family's survival, but I needed time to get in the right frame of mind. I sat like a butterfly spreading its wings to gather strength for flight, closing my eyes and feeling the warmth of the rising sun soak deeply into my skin.

––––––

Government bureaucrats didn't recognize Dad's pre-communist land title as rightful ownership, so they did not approve of him hiring laborers. But in spite of this, the harvesting crew he employed averaged eight to ten people, a mixture of family and gypsies. The core crew consisted of the entire Cismigiu household: Dad and Mom, Marin, Lenuṭa, and me. Dad often employed relatives and gypsies living nearby in need of money, and three gypsies were onsite this morning.

These gypsies were loyal to my father because he had a reputation for treating them with respect. It was no secret that several gypsies often could be found in our farm field. When the gypsies were questioned as to why they were in our tomato field or on our farm, they knew to say that they were simply helping a friend.

The government did not allow gypsies to own land, which limited what food they could self-produce. Many were migratory, others squatters living in makeshift shacks on tracts of land set aside by the government.

The authorities and police were a mixture of personalities with varying intentions. Some were staunchly aligned with the brutality of the Communist regime, enjoying their power to take advantage of others—even when these others were former friends, schoolmates, and neighbors. But among them were individuals who had simply signed allegiance to the Communist Party for self-preservation. These kind-hearted souls turned a blind eye to the fact that my father employed family and friends. They understood that he was helping others survive, putting food on their tables and hope in their hearts. These neighbors and community members respected him for doing so when they didn't have the courage or opportunity.

Dad paid gypsies fifty *lei* per day. One family with three to four members working could make 150-200 *lei* per day, but they might not have work every day.

Gypsies might be secretly wealthy (or at least assumed to be) in many other parts of the world, but we knew these gypsies on a personal level, and they indeed had a meager existence as compared to most other Romanians. This is why they were appreciative and loyal to my parents and had been to my grandparents as well. Some people tolerate diversity, but my parents fostered it. They saw the good in everyone.

———

I heard footsteps to my left coming around the corner of the house and opened my eyes to see our trusted gypsy worker, Pavel, and four of his friends and relatives walking in single file behind him. He waved, and I flashed a smile and nodded in return. Gypsies were routinely hired to weed, plant, and harvest, and Pavel was a faithful and frequent assistant around our farm. He came almost every day to help with something. He was considered family. From a distance, one might mistake him for my father, as they were about the same height and both had dark hair, but Pavel was darker skinned and sported a mustache.

One gypsy colony was located behind my grandparents' home in the next town, so my father and Pavel had known each other as kids. Pavel was allowed to borrow our horse and wagon to haul firewood to his home, and he never took the privilege for granted. He always showed up the following day, whether asked to work or not, wanting to help with some task, any task, to show his gratitude.

I rose from the beam of sunshine where I sat at the back door and followed the gypsies to the greenhouse. Dad was coordinating and communicating how the assembly line of restoration would take place. All hands were on deck to receive instructions: Mom, Marin, Lenuța, five gypsies, and me. Maybe others saw this as a good form of exercise or a means to make money, but the morning shadows cast a gloomy spell over me. The cloudless sky and still air promised an uncomfortable day in the dirt.

The restoration of the fields could be usually accomplished in one day. Simi and Dad would restore the labyrinth of irrigation trenches. The replanting crew came immediately behind and groomed the botanical dressing by restoring salvageable plants, and removing and replacing those that had been destroyed.

Watching Dad and Simi walk through the field restoring the former beauty of design was like viewing a movie clip played backward with irrigation trenches and planting mounds rolling out from under the double-blade plow, contoured as they were before. Their synchronized movements were graceful.

The assembly line that followed had a person with a pick shovel poking a hole spaced evenly apart on one side of each mounded row. This placement aided the irrigation by locating the roots closer to the moisture when the trenches were soaked with water.

I wheelbarrowed tomato plants from the greenhouse, dropping a plastic-encased plant next to each hole.

Next came a hired gypsy, crawling down the row, kicking up dust. He removed the root ball from its container, leaving a trail of discarded plastic sheaths, then widened the hole in the dirt mound with his free hand, inserted the tomato plant, and firmed the soil to support it.

I circled back and picked up the plastic sheaths. My hands were small and the rows long, so I shoved them into my pockets and inside my T-shirt and emptied them into a large burlap bag at far-end of the field. I ended up with more dirt inside than outside my clothes.

————

With ten people on work duty, including Dad working the horse and plow, there were three replanting teams of three people each. By sunset we were done. Dad and stallion were streaked with rivulets of sweat dusted with dirt, and the hands of the planting crew were stained dark hunter green from handling so much tomato foliage.

My muscles ached and my body cried for a bath and bed, but I always felt a sense of satisfaction and accomplishment at the day's end. A beautiful transformation took place each planting. It was amazing to see the black field of the morning turned to a field of lush green by evening. The smell of raw earth lingered in my nostrils, enriching my awareness of how vital the mineral-laced soil was to the growth of my father's prized tomatoes.

We started the irrigation pump, letting it run slowly all night. The plants thrived in the warm soil with abundant moisture. In the morning, it was encouraging to see the overnight change and the spurt of growth.

————

Father's technique of pruning tomato plants maximized production by encouraging growth to produce a strong center shaft with shortened branches so that very little foliage was shown. The result was that by harvest time it produced what looked like a stack of red clustery grapes with tomatoes the size of large grapefruit.

Posts were staked six feet apart with a break between each thirty-foot sectional plot in the row where the water trough from the center cut across to the edge of the field. Each mounded row of tomato plants was trellised with three support wires strung taut between them, to which the tomato plants were secured as they reached for the sky. This was not done until the plants grew to a good height but before the tomatoes formed to a size that could topple the plant.

This is why the police raid, which always came soon after the initial planting, had luckily not damaged any of these support structures.

――――

Springtime melted into the heat of summer, and our second-chance tomato planting seemed to be a gamble that once again might pay off in a good harvest.

Farmers fear natural disasters from the moment of planting seed until crops are harvested and sold, but I witnessed my parents bearing an extra load of worry. They were fearful that the police might make this year the first year to strike twice. They say lightning rarely strikes the same place more than once, but I remember my parents' worried reaction every time storm clouds rolled in. Even the natural disaster potential was an eerie reminder of the sinister communist behavior that might strike again without warning.

10

A Kid's Life

~ Summer 1982 ~

WHAT comes to mind when I think of "summer"?

> *There are sights and sounds, and merry-go-rounds.*
> *There are vacations and places to be.*
> *There are movies and laughing and swimming hole splashing.*
> *There are days filled with gladness and glee.*

> *To me it was pick'n and not the guitar,*
> *But tomatoes that weighed by the ton.*
> *There was work at first sunlight that lingered 'til midnight,*
> *And the farm chores to always be done.*

I liked the break from school, but my favorite season was not what might be expected from a child. It might have been summertime, if circumstances had been different.

Summer break from school was June 15 to September 15, but it was not a break for summer fun. It was a break to work. Summertime, for my siblings and me, meant working hard in the field rather than a life of leisure.

My parents would understandably hate to see hail and storms damage the tomato crop, but by the time school started again, I dreamt of the possibility. My brother, sister, and I did not play with other children during our summer school break. We were not afforded vacations to exotic destinations, or even simple excursions or visits to relatives. Tomato farming, with its relentless needs, was not much fun.

Tomatoes were our lifeline, and lifelines come with responsibilities. There was never a question of why we needed to help make ends meet. Marin, Lenuța, and I had adult responsibilities, but we were still kids.

Marin and I were fortunate to have Lenuța for our sister. When we got into trouble, she cried in our defense. And when given the opportunity, she picked the hardest chores, leaving Marin and me with the easier ones.

Our parents tried to shield us from the harsh realities of a repressive regime by not complaining too much in our presence, but the toll on Romanian society could not be hidden, and the weight of communism crushed the spirit. Everyone carried a burden of uncertainty, but it was actually a privilege living on a farm in a rural part of the country, where sustainability was part of everyday life.

Mother was in charge of managing the majority of the farm crew, including the hired help. She was better at it than my father. Mother always included the five immediate family members in the total count of workers needed. In fact, the three of us children had seniority for inclusion whether we wanted it or not. Mother should get credit for creating one of the first "right-to-work" laws. It was "right" for her children to work on the farm and "wrong" for them to refuse.

———

For those who have never farmed—never planted thousands of tomato plants in one year in one field—it might be difficult to imagine the work involved to ensure a bountiful harvest. I was there every day, and my sore-muscles made the memory more vivid.

Summer was the sting of sweat in my eyes and taste of salt on my tongue. Perspiration beaded on my forehead in drops so large that the dust scattered when droplets fell and hit the dry ground. I often wondered if tomato plant growth was inhibited or enhanced by the saltiness of my sweat. We always had a bountiful harvest, so evidently the plants thrived on sodium.

I tried to keep the dirt on my fingers away from my face, but invariably when I wiped the perspiration tickling my forehead and running down my cheeks, I ended up smearing mud across my face, even when using my forearm. It's a wonder I did not end up with sunburnt zebra streaks, but the intensity of the sun penetrated dirt. Over the summer season, my skin transformed into worn leather with dark desert hues.

I was torn about whether to wear my hair long or short in summer. Long hair was a layered protection from the ultraviolet sunrays, but when soaked with perspiration, it acted as a dust collector, matting grit against the scalp and skin. Short hair spared that sensation but resulted in my head getting hot. I had too much pride to wear a hat, so I opted most often for the shaggier look.

I found it easier to crawl in the dry trench than to bend over to reach under the tomato plants to pull weeds. The sun-soaked soil was hot and the dust I kicked up as I scooted along clouded the air I breathed.

After we weeded rows of soil mounds by hand, Dad weeded the troughs using a single-blade plow pulled behind his beloved and talented stallion. Dad positioned Simi at the start of a row, and Simi looked back over his shoulder as if to confirm Dad was ready and holding the reins. Seemingly satisfied, Simi stepped forward with the grace and control of a balance beam gymnast.

The stallion's hindquarters filled the width of the row, but Simi avoided rubbing the plants and bruising the tomatoes. He stepped over any mounds of soil at the end of each section, and Dad lifted up the plow at the same place, as the duo marched down a row, softening and weeding the soil in the trough. The field was now ready for irrigation.

Irrigating was one chore I had reason to enjoy even though the preparation for it was a lot of work. Irrigation began by pumping water into the trough furrowed down the center of the field. As the water gently filled and flowed, we diverted it to the right and left of the center trough by damming dirt at the end of each row. This allowed each to fill, and the water to soak into the ground. The process was slowly repeated as we moved across the field from front to back until the soil in each section was saturated.

Dad did not like pesticides or chemical fertilizers but used natural methods to promote growth. Periodically, he fertilized the field by putting chicken manure in the trough at the beginning of the irrigation process.

My fun began when I was waiting for a section to be flooded and the troughs flowed with water. I launched a boat race. I cut a cucumber in half and scooped out most of the contents, leaving the green shell and a small chunk in the center to which I inserted a makeshift sail. My play took me on schooners sailing the Seven Seas.

––––––

Summertime sights and sounds may be universal to some extent, but my recollection of a few in particular is less of romp and more of restraint.

About once every two weeks, an ice cream truck with a loudspeaker mounted on top drove through town and around the neighboring countryside. It broadcast that a movie would be played in the town center community building on a given night, normally a Friday or Saturday.

Movie theaters were more prevalent in big cities, but our small town contained no such luxury. The town center community building, where weddings were sometimes conducted, did have theater-style seating and served as a makeshift movie house for these occasions.

We begged our parents to let us go. Dad was more inclined to grant permission from the start, or at least it seemed so, because he would say, "Go ask your mother." If we could convince her, then permission was granted. But confirmation was never obtained until the last minute.

Mom must have felt more panic to get the farm work done. Mom was a better manager than Dad, but we were not looking for a manager. We were looking for a liberator.

On the final day before movie showtime, my brother, sister, and I begged with greater intensity. Mom never gave us leave until the last minute. It seems like the principles of psychology might have produced better results if Mom had divulged her intentions hours earlier. We would have been much more productive in the tomato field by not wasting so much effort pleading. When she finally gave the green light, the race was on.

Many owned bicycles and rode them everywhere: to get a loaf of bread at the store, to pick up medicine at the pharmacy, to get from point A to point B. In Grandpa's era, the specialty bikes were from Germany, but as far back as I remember, there were two choices: Romanian or Russian. The Russian bikes were most coveted, built strong and rugged. Most families had one bike of some sort, but Dad always owned at least three—all Russian-made.

Rarely were all three bikes available because Dad often loaned them out. When only one bicycle was accessible, my brother allowed my sister to sit on the seat while he peddled, and the two took off, leaving me to run the entire way to town center without stopping. I should have been a marathon or speed runner with as much practice as I got. I kept pace with my brother's bike most of the way. Out of breath, but full of excitement, we all too often arrived at the moment the movie started.

Each movie showing was a packed house. It seemed the whole town showed up—young and old.

Seating stretched beyond the theater chairs in all directions. Children of all ages sat on the floor in between the first row of seating and the movie screen. Of course, the motion picture was blurrier at close distance, and our necks ached afterward from the strain, but that was a price far less to pay than that of missing the film altogether.

There was a balcony on either side of the movie projector box. It only had standing room, with the rear row of standees leaning against the back wall and everyone else leaning on each other.

Dust filtered through the projector light like gnats swarming in the summer sun. Constant clicking from the projector and the noise of the spinning reel produced a rhythmic backdrop to every soundtrack.

Each movie came mounted on multiple reels, and some of the film was split and spliced or brittle from overuse. When either the end of the film rolled through the projector or split prematurely, there was sudden silence from the soundtrack, followed by a collective moan from the audience as bright light flashed against the movie screen and bounced back into our eyes. The projectionist never responded fast enough, as the film end flapped and spun, sounding like a playing card stuck in the spoke of a bicycle wheel.

The movies were of East Indian origin, maybe because they were cheaper and easier to obtain or maybe to keep us from seeing the American lifestyle. It was ironic that people in India probably watched American films, while we in Romania watched Indian films.

———

There was something more maddening than missing movies, however. We knew movies were sporadic and not a daily enticement, but the lure of laughing and splashing from the river was enough to drive me insane with envy on a daily basis.

The Bârlad River flows cool and clear, hugging the outskirts of our hometown. About a half-mile from our farm, a bridge was built to access the farmland on the other side. I am not sure who originally built it, but it was not maintained by the Department of Transportation. Men living in the area, like my father, used their own tools to help preserve it. The bridge was large enough for horse-drawn carts and pedestrians. There were only fields on the opposite side, so there was no need for vehicles to pass over the river at this particular point.

The river was deep so the bridge was an ideal diving and jumping platform for summertime swims. Kids jumping off the bridge at random looked like mass cluster bombs plummeting into the water. From a distance, it looked like controlled chaos, but there was no one in control. No lifeguard helped manage the mayhem.

The shrills and thrills from every kid in the vicinity skipped across the water and echoed in our ears as my sister, brother, and I labored in the summertime sun in the middle of the tomato field.

The sound drove us crazy. It was torture—not the fact that they were swimming, but that we were not.

We begged Mom for permission to swim every hot summer day. We were like fish out of water, moping and flopping around, wasting energy complaining about not swimming that should have been directed toward doing our chores.

Unlike the fish who finally succumbs and ends up quietly lying still in the dirt, our pleas for leniency and our tactics to wear our mom's tolerance thin intensified as the afternoon wore on. Mom was afraid of the water because she couldn't swim, which caused her to be extra hesitant, but eventually she gave us fifteen minutes leave of absence.

I was a quick learner. It didn't take long for me to realize that if I put on my swimsuit under my pants before I headed to the tomato field to work, then precious moments were saved by stripping out of my work attire while running to the river. It was easy to pull off my shirt and throw it somewhere alongside the road to be retrieved on the way home. Because time was of the essence when going to the river, I didn't hesitate to plunge right in and remove any remaining clothes in the water. I felt justified in thinking I was pre-washing my clothes to help Mom.

It took less than three minutes to run to the river. But it took longer to get back because that eagerness had left us. That left only ten minutes for swimming.

Running barefoot on the road to the swimming hole was possible for two reasons: my feet were calloused from working barefoot in the field, and the pain of pebbles was always less than the pain of being deprived the river.

We did not dip our toes in the water to test the temperature—we plunged right in, squealing at top lung capacity to harmonize with the others already in concert.

And we always forgot about the time—always—until we saw our mother riding the bike and carrying an extra-long branch. It looked like a car antenna whipping in the wind.

We scrambled up the riverbank, not taking time to dry off (we didn't bring towels anyway), and started running like rabbits toward home. We ran without looking back, mere steps ahead of Mom shouting her frustration about our lack of attention, not keeping time, not obeying her. The noise of her yelling allowed us to know which side of the road to dart to for protection as we kept close to the fence line to escape the swing of the branch in her hand.

We ran straight to the field, still in our swimming suits, and immediately began working as if we had never left. We continued to listen to her rant about our unacceptable behavior, but we focused more on the distant sound of the kids splashing in the river. We relished the memory of the cool water, the brief moments of reprieve from the summer heat, and the dream that we would be swimming again tomorrow.

But tomorrow's swim usually took about three days to arrive until our mother's wrath abated.

———

As an adult, I can appreciate the burden our mother felt for coordinating the volume of work that had to be done. She had a mother's heart, and it must have pained her to force her children's attention to chores instead of childhood pleasures. Perhaps that is why she allowed us to whine so loudly for so long without reprimanding us. She let us vent, but surely the sound of our distress stung. It likely pained her more than it pained us to deny swimming privileges or movie passes. She knew there was more at stake. Our very existence depended upon this cash crop. This was our lot in life—a lot of limitations, and a lot of work.

11

First Harvest

~ Summer 1982 ~

THE ready-to-harvest tomatoes, patterned across the field, looked like artistry painted on canvas. Deep green stalks reached for the sky, and leaves cupped the warmth of the sun. Tomatoes of all sizes in varying shades of green and red hung from stems like Christmas tree ornaments.

Nothing had been left to chance, except for the weather. Every detail had been planned: seed selection, soil preparation, timing of planting, nurturing, and now the harvesting and transporting of the tomatoes to market.

The weather was warm, the days long, and our spirits full of energy. Come September, when the harvest season would be winding down, the weather would be cooler, the days shorter, and our spirits lagging. But the hired help and family members were eager to begin. Dad was not the only one who savored the first harvest day; each of the picking crew shared in the sense of pride and accomplishment of what the harvest meant for their sustenance.

———

The luscious red tomatoes would be picked every three to four days as they ripened in the summer sun. The tomato picking started immediately after breakfast. We ate earlier on harvest days so work could begin soon after daybreak.

The first harvest of the summer, in early July, was always exciting; everyone seemed eager to get outside and enjoy the weather. The toils of the previous year's harvest were a distant memory, having faded with time over the long fall and winter. Spring had ushered in a feeling of freshness, a new beginning that was bearing fruit of labor. The plowing and planting, the weeding and tending, produced the ripened prospect of harvest now within grasp.

Each picker was given a five-gallon bucket. One would start working at one side of the field, and the others would just take up in the row next to someone else.

Dad picked tomatoes faster than anyone while at the same time observing the crew to ensure proper handling. He took pride in every aspect of the process—growing, picking, packing, transporting, and selling the most beautiful tomatoes. His tomatoes looked picture perfect.

The early morning dew would cling like liquid pearls to the tomato plants. The sun could later evaporate these droplets, but that seldom happened. Most of the dew brushed off on our clothing as we walked a row. The coolness of the dew was a welcome sensation in the hot afternoon blaze, but it was not as pleasant in the damp cool mornings. No one seemed to mind this as much as me, probably because I was the youngest and shortest, and the dew droplets made a muddier mess of my shirt, pants, and toes. Or at least, I thought so.

The tomatoes were transferred from the five-gallon buckets into wheelbarrows or, when there was an extra helping hand, a person was assigned to bring empty buckets to the pickers in exchange for their full ones. Someone would either carry two buckets at a time back to the barn or push the wheelbarrow once it was full. The tomatoes were carefully piled in the barn to protect them from the heat and to prepare for later crating.

––––––

Mom sent Lenuța to the house around ten-thirty to start preparing lunch for the crew. I was jealous this was not my assigned task. Lenuța did not have to start the entire meal from scratch. Mom often cooked in quantity, late into the night, or woke up early to prepare food.

Breakfast seemed like a distant memory. I welcomed the shout from Lenuța that lunch was ready.

The entire picking crew was invited into the house for lunch. Lunch usually included a noodle sour-broth soup, either beef or chicken, full of vegetables and a healthy dose of parsley. Today was no exception.

Steam rose from the bowls at each place setting when we arrived in the kitchen. The soup, called *borș*, was soothing and refreshing, even though served hot during the summer. The herbs and spices lingered on my taste buds a good while into the afternoon.

The soup was served first, followed by a simple salad: a variety of cucumbers, onions, and—of course—fresh tomatoes, all drizzled with olive oil, salt, and red wine vinegar. Cold cuts and cheese provided protein for the final course.

Muscles not used to the activity ached since it was the first morning of the first harvest of the season. We ate with haste and without much talking. No one ate fast just for the privilege of heading back to the field, but all understood the reality of the sun moving across the sky. It had not paused for lunch, and there were many more tomatoes to pick while it was yet light.

One by one, the picking crew excused themselves from the lunch table and headed back to the field. Dad was the first. I was the last. Lenuța hurried me out of the house by threatening me with cleanup duty. But she quickly cleaned the kitchen and prepared for the evening meal before rejoining the picking crew in the field.

———

The afternoon seemed to drag on longer than the morning, even though it had been interrupted by the lunch break.

Afternoon clouds rolled over the distant Carpathian mountaintops. While no one spoke it out loud, the common thought— more like a silent prayer—was that these clouds would provide a few refreshing droplets of heavenly water or at least a moment of shade. But the clouds often dissolved into the atmosphere before reaching us and our sunbaked tomato field.

At midafternoon, Mom often would tell me to run and fetch drinking water for the crew. Heat waves danced in the field beneath the sweltering sun as it seemed to hover without movement in the cloudless sky. My throat was as dry as dust, not to mention that I relished any excuse to get out of the field. I darted toward the well, knowing the sooner I drew the water, the sooner I could relieve my parched mouth.

———

Good water meant good luck. When my parents built our home, they dug two wells, one outside the front gate next to the road and the other behind our house between the barn and the tomato field. The well near the road was a common tradition that ensured passersby could freely get a cool drink. This was an act of kindness believed to bring prosperity and good fortune. Dad and Mom thought it was healthier to have a "live" well, so they chose to dip it by hand rather than install indoor plumbing for drinking water.

It still fascinates me how these wells were commonly constructed. A large concrete tube about four feet high and four feet in diameter was positioned on the ground, and the dirt on the inside bottom was dug out by hand using a shovel until the heavy cylinder slid and shifted its way downward. This process of digging and removing the dirt from the inside bottom ring continued until the top of the cylinder was ground level. One cylinder after another was placed on top and the routine repeated until water was found.

Building a well was at least a two-man job, and the hired diggers had a skill that was traditionally handed down through their family. This was not an artesian well, but as the digger neared the water table, he had to coordinate with his crew above ground to extract the muddy mess using buckets on ropes.

When the water flowed clear, the digger would climb out using a rope ladder. A decorative cylinder was then hoisted on top and a pitched roof built to cover and protect the well from the rain and sunlight.

———

I stopped by and retrieved the porcelain water pail sitting on a stool in the kitchen and hurried through the front gate to the well by the road. I planted the pail on the level ground to keep it from tipping as I filled it.

A rustic, weathered wooden bucket sat on the well ledge. Bands of metal, oxidized reddish-brown, ringed the top and bottom of the tongue-and-grooved wood slats, tightening them in place.

I swung the bucket-on-a-chain into the well opening and allowed the chain to slip through my hands as it spun around the water wheel pulley. The bucket splashed into the water below, tipping and filling quickly. Pulling with alternating hands, I lifted the bucket brimming with water, the chain coiling at my feet with each yank. Droplets sloshed from the bucket rim echoing, like raindrops as they hit the surface below. I poured the cold, fresh water into the five-gallon pail and repeated the process until it was full.

I left the bucket on the well ledge and hurried back to the field as fast as a ten-year-old could carry five gallons of sloshing liquid.

———

Picking stopped around six, but much work still needed to be done.

As most of the crew began the next phase of the process, Mom and Lenuța headed to the house to prepare dinner. There was little time to eat because of all the work still ahead, but Mom and Dad knew a harvest crew must be well-fed.

Dad threw the barn doors open wide to take advantage of all the natural daylight still possible, and it looked impressive to see the day's tomato harvest piled in mounds that stretched across the barn floor. Each had been stacked in about the same height so as not to bruise the tomatoes on the bottom.

Crewmembers grabbed a stack of wooden crates, wooden lids, and newspapers and then knelt before a tomato mound to start the crating process. Marin darted back into the barn sloshing two brimming water buckets. He had retrieved a stack of clean cloths from Mom at the house, and he dipped several into the water pails, wrung them out, and then handed everyone a damp cloth to wipe the tomatoes clean. We carefully placed around forty kilos of tomatoes into each crate.

I knelt on the floor next to my chosen tomato mountain and lined the crate with several sheets of newspaper to protect the tomatoes from the rough wooden slats. I picked up the first tomato, wiped it with the damp cloth, and arranged it inside the crate. Dad had taught us how to stack the tomatoes in rows so they would not bruise by either being too tightly or too loosely packed. I took pride and care in this particular task almost as much as Dad did.

Dad made the final inspection of each crate when it was stacked full, then fitted the wooden lid on top, fastening the four corners with short pieces of steel wire. For the second magical time of the day, the call to eat coming from the house broke the monotony of the moment. The crating of tomatoes might be done before midnight, but during the height of the harvest season, we expected to stay up much later.

As the last glow of sunlight flared from the red-stained sunset, I walked with Dad, Marin, and the remaining harvest crew from the barn to the farmhouse. Dinner's aroma floated through the open kitchen window into the evening air with an intensity I could taste.

The flavored bouquet of hot salted pork fat infused with the sweet tang of minced garlic and caramelized onion was undoubtedly *sarmale* simmering on the stove, which is a blend of minced pork, tomato sauce, dill, parsley, onion, salt, pepper, and rice. These ingredients are sautéed for stuffing into preserved grape leaves or rolled into blanched cabbage leaves, which I found irresistible when served with the staple of boiled yellow cornmeal, called *mămăligă*.

The hint of fresh cheese melting in boiled corn flour would unmistakably be our *polenta*—another staple in place of bread. I also whiffed fresh dough being deep-fried in oil to make donuts. I hoped my nose was not failing me.

Grocery stores were common for people living in the city, but we butchered our own meat, ground kernels into flour and meal, pressed oil from sunflower seeds, and bought milk from a neighbor until we had our own milk cow. Butter, cheese, sour cream, and yogurt—made at home—were always fresh and creamy.

MARK LEE MYERS

One might like to enjoy a bath before supper, but a bath was not an amenity afforded right now because bed was not going to be an after-dinner luxury. Everyone sighed as the weight of the day lifted when we sank into our chairs. It was good to sit down and wiggle our toes.

Steam misted up from the hot dishes on the table, and my eyes darted to each one. I had correctly identified the aromas.

Scattered between the hot dishes were fresh, raw garden vegetables, including carrots, onions, and, no surprise again, sliced tomatoes sprinkled with salt and pepper. Water had been poured into drinking glasses in front of each plate, and pitchers of our house wine graced the table at each end. Even we children were allowed a small portion of watered-down wine.

There was always plenty of food but rarely any leftovers. The dog seldom feasted from the crumbs of our table.

Dinnertime was a special time of the day, and the meals during early harvest were almost like a holiday. The conversation would be on the harvest, but it was not a tale of tiring toil. It was laughter and celebration.

Dad asked everyone to guess the weight of the first day's harvest. He always had an advantage, which came from his years of experience.

I was no competition as a ten-year-old. I tried to relate the tomato piles to something of similar size. I had no idea. I should have counted the number of peaks in the sea of tomato waves before the crating process began.

How many wooden crates might each mound fill? It seemed like three or four. This would have been an easy way to calculate a guess. Now, with this contest already in play, it was too late. I had not counted the piles when I had the chance. But I was trying to be too scientific. It was a lighthearted contest.

Dad had not weighed the bounty, but his authoritative answer was never questioned. The winner was the person who guessed a weight closest to Dad's estimate.

After dinner, we resumed crating tomatoes in the barn, and, as often was the case in the early part of the harvest season, we would finish before midnight. I could hardly envision the extra work that lay ahead when we would harvest three metric tons at each picking.

I'd never had a headache before, but one started developing now. My ten-year-old body ached in several places. I looked at my father. His clothes were as dirty as everyone else's, and his face was also stained by sweat. But he did not appear exhausted.

Mom directed me to a quick bath the moment I stepped back inside the house. Normally, I executed delaying tactics but not tonight. I was tired to the bone. But I was also excited about tomorrow's trip to market with Dad, and I slid into bed, hoping to drift asleep before my head hit the pillow or before I could start counting sheep—or tomatoes.

12

Midnight Wagon

~ Summer 1982 ~

I DIDN'T hear the rooster call at daybreak. But when Mom shook my shoulder lightly, I jumped right out of bed.

I was excited about a long-anticipated journey, the first of my lifetime. Time would be spent making last-minute preparations—including an afternoon nap—for the overnight trek. There would be no sleeping en route.

The previous day's harvest yielded more than half a metric ton of tomatoes, which was small in comparison to what the field would produce later in the season. But a half metric ton of ripe tomatoes was too much supply for the limited demand from the neighboring communities. The fertile Siret Valley and neighboring rural area was mostly farmland, so folks had their own gardens and grew their own fruits and vegetables.

Communist rules dictated that individuals could sell their garden produce only within the tight vicinity of where it was grown. The rule did not allow transport outside the county. But adherence to this rule would prevent our survival. Dad had no choice but to find customers in a city toward the nearby Carpathian foothills to the west. It was not profitable to attempt transporting this small first harvest of the season to a place very far away.

Dad chose to market his first tomato crops of the season in Focşani, a small mountain city thirty-five miles away in the next county. He had made this same trip for many years now, and today was the first time I would join him on the journey. The trip to Focşani took an hour in a motorized vehicle, but Dad did not own one. He simply had a great horse and a wagon.

There were good two-lane roads accessing Focşani, but the risk of exposure was too great to travel this distance by horse and wagon on the roads. Not only would there be a problem at the county border crossing, but one never knew when a random official would choose to harass and hinder the journey en route. Dad had found a shortcut using old dirt paths and trails over the hills and through the forest to avoid detection.

The trip to the Focşani market would commence after nightfall for two reasons: to time arrival at the open market early morning and to prevent drawing attention.

I loved it—an adventure!

———

Dinner was ready earlier than usual, and Dad, Marin, and I ate quickly. There was no lighthearted conversation like other nights. Immediately after eating, the three of us were excused from the table, and Marin and I were relieved of any cleanup chores in the kitchen.

In the barn, Dad hitched Simi to the wagon, and we began to load it. Marin and I grabbed the opposite sides of a tomato crate, lifting it between us. As we neared the wagon, we swung the crate upward, landing it gently at Dad's feet. Dad then stacked and secured the crates in place. I was glad for Marin's help, but I would be traveling alone with Dad, and I wondered if Dad expected me to unload the crates by myself when we got to market.

The sun dipped below the horizon and the afterglow colored the high-altitude wispy clouds in the west as we finished loading the wagon. I ran back to the house and darted to my bedroom. I had almost forgotten my pocketknife. I did not keep it on display. My parents had warned me that the police would confiscate it if found during one of the routine police raids in our home. I had it well hidden between the mattress and bed slat. I grasped the pocketknife tightly in my palm, holding it a happy moment and shoving it deep into my pants pocket.

I saw my parents embrace in a tight hug as I neared the barn. Dad lifted her head from his shoulder and smiled reassuringly into her eyes. Mom's lips were not moving, but I could see concern in her solemn expression.

Maybe mothers worried too much. Mine was always telling me, "You be careful, Son!" I assumed that was what all mothers said. Surely, she did not need to tell Dad something similar. He could handle anything.

As I neared my parents, I heard Dad say, "Plan for the worst—hope for the best." *What was there to worry about?*

———

Our one-horse wagon headed north on the dirt path toward Umbrăreşti, then turned westward before reaching the outskirts of town and heading in the direction of Condrea. We rattled over a rickety wooden bridge spanning the Bârlad River.

Circumventing Condrea on the south side and heading northwest, we traversed the good grassland of the bucolic terrain. Sheepherders pastured their flocks in the expanse. Wherever there were sheep, there was a sheepdog, and wherever a sheepdog, we heard a barrage of barking as our wagon rolled and rocked through the night.

I stretched out on a blanket spread on top of the wooden tomato crates. I was not sleepy, but lying down allowed me to view the stars, and they were especially bright on this cloudless, moonless night.

After a good distance of travel, while still staring at the stars, I had a strange sensation. "Dad?" I queried, "Are we—moving—BACKward?"

"Nooo ...," Dad drawled. "Have you been dreaming? You have been quiet for some time."

"I'm not dreaming, Dad. I am not sleepy and have not slept. I am lying here gazing at the stars. I've been focused on them for a long time—and then all of a sudden, I got the sensation the wagon was moving backward. Really strange!"

"Well, first of all, my son, we are definitely still moving forward. Simi is a great horse and can do many things other horses can't do, but he can't trot backward as fast as we are moving forward." It was too dark for me to see Dad's grin, but I could hear it in his voice.

"I'm serious. It really looked like it and felt like it, too," I insisted.

"I've actually had that same sensation," Dad admitted.

"When?"

"I was riding in a wagon coming back from town with your grandpa, and I was doing the same thing as you—staring at the stars. I don't remember telling Grandpa, but I do remember wondering what might have caused it. I think the brain gets tricked or confused at what we are seeing and it makes us feel a weird sensation as it tries to sort it all out."

"Did you see that?" I shouted.

"A falling star!" Dad and I said the same words at the same time. We both had seen it. The brilliance of white had streaked from the heavens behind us and lingered as it trailed off far in front of us.

"That was amazing. I have never seen one with a tail that long or bright," I said.

"It did light up the sky. That was a good show, and it headed straight in the direction we are going. Can you see the forest up ahead?"

I sat up instantly, kneeling on my blanket and bracing myself against the wagon seat. I squinted hard, disappointed I could not see the silhouette of trees but only darkness.

I had played in the woods near our home, but never too often at night. And those were smaller patches of trees. I had also gone into the woods to help Dad scoop up soil for the greenhouses and to gather firewood, but that again was always during the day and never too far from home. On this journey, I was excited about traveling through the larger forest; this was my first time to see it, but there was not much to see at this moment.

Dad sensed my struggle. "It looks a whole lot different in the daytime. We will ride through the trees with a little daylight to our advantage on the return trip. It's too dark to see much tonight, but do you see where the darker shadows are on the horizon?"

MARK LEE MYERS

"I think so," I said. "Yeah ... I see it now. So how will we get through it?" I was not aware of this hurdle before now. "It is dark and there are no roads."

"There are paths, sort of like roads," Dad explained. "The Germans cut these paths through the woods during World War II so they could move their army tanks and equipment more easily. They are not used much anymore, especially at night, so we won't have any congestion on this road tonight." He chuckled.

"How will Simi know the way?" I asked. Dad had traded for Simi the previous fall, so this was our stallion's first trip to market.

"Once we find the opening, the horse will lead the way. I may not even have to hold the reins. Simi is the best horse in the world. But first," he said, sitting taller on the wagon seat, "before we get to the forest, we must cross a wide river."

I had also not thought of this. I knew of the river near Tecuci, many miles north of home, which we had crossed on occasion. Maybe it was the same river, but on the road, there was a bridge.

"Is there a bridge?"

"No bridge," Dad said, matter of fact. "But there is a boat. It's called a barge. It's big enough to hold the horse and wagon, and it will take us to the other side."

This all seemed mysterious to me, but if Dad was not worried, neither was I. Well, maybe a little bit.

———

Simi sensed the water long before those of us sitting on the wagon seat did. The horse could smell it, and I felt the slight change in how he trotted. At first, he seemed to pull harder as if wanting to get there faster. He no doubt was thirsty, as there had not been any water to drink since we left the barn.

I saw starlight flickering on the river, and then a skiff of clouds floated overhead. Simi must have seen the same; his attitude changed. He was a fearless stallion by day, but I felt there was something fearful in the horse now, an uneasy feeling as we approached the swift current of the river by night.

Dad spoke softly to his horse. "It's all right, Simi. Just ease on up, my friend." He spoke with a calm and reassuring voice. It was in the same voice he always spoke to Simi. His voice comforted and calmed me now as well.

The river looming before us was called the Siret. The current was rushing, racing to merge with the Danube and eventually discharge into the Black Sea. We could hear it now. Simi trusted his master, but the horse was still nervous.

"Hello there," Dad bellowed.

"Hello." The barge captain must have recognized Dad's voice from the many times he had come this way before.

Dad nudged the horse to step closer, but Simi had gone as close as he would with his master behind him. He would go no closer until his master led him. Dad handed me the reins and stepped down from the wagon.

"Hold these loosely," he whispered. "I will lead him to the water's edge."

That seemed like a great idea to me because I could not see the water's edge, though I could hear it lapping against the riverbank. No wonder the horse was spooked. I had never felt Simi react this way. I was holding the reins "loosely" as Dad had instructed. *Surely tense horse muscles can't be felt through these thin reins,* I thought. But I felt tension.

I took a deep breath and exhaled slowly, trying to relax, knowing Dad was now confidently leading us both to the river's edge. I felt the muscle tension ease and realized it had not been the horse. It was my own muscles that had been tense.

Cosmic light filtered through the wispy cloud cover, silhouetting our shapes.

"You have a new horse," the captain observed.

"A stallion worth more than two," Dad opined.

"You also have a new rider."

"My youngest son, Nicolae," Dad introduced. "Nicolae, this is Sandu, our barge captain."

MARK LEE MYERS

I started to raise my hand to wave and immediately realized the movement may not be detectable. "Hello," I said.

"Good to meet you," Sandu replied.

The barge was old—a simple floating platform with no rails. It could hold about three small cars in length, but it was not made for cars, and I questioned if it would be strong and sturdy enough for this one horse and tomato wagon.

There were no lights, but Sandu and Dad knew where to step. Sandu gave approval to step aboard, and Dad tugged on Simi's bridle harness.

Simi flung his head back and jerked the wagon. I grabbed for anything in the darkness to keep from falling off. Perhaps I had relaxed too much.

Simi stepped on the barge and I felt the platform sink into the water. Simi hesitated once again, and Dad whispered in his ear and kept a tight hold on the bridle harness. Simi moved slowly forward, and his massive weight started to balance out on the platform.

The wagon wheels were still on the riverbank. Simi needed to pull forward a little farther. If Simi spooked now, there were no rails to keep him from plunging into the water off the front of the barge. Rails or no rails, it really did not matter. The weight of the horse, wagon, and load of tomato crates would not restrain Simi if he bolted forward.

Dad continued guiding and coaxing Simi to take those last few steps forward by faith, and Simi tugged one last time, bringing the wagon rocking onto the barge. The platform wobbled and creaked, and it seemed that everyone—Sandu, Dad, Simi, and I—held our breath. The platform settled and we exhaled in relief.

Sandu untied the barge from its anchor point, and shoved off using a wooden oar. There was no motor to propel the barge forward. Sandu did it mostly by hand, dipping the oar into the black water. The barge platform was attached to a cable that stretched across the river, but I could not see more than a few feet of it as it was lost in the blackness of the night.

As Sandu moved the barge farther from shore, the river's current caught the platform and propelled our floating shadows faster into the blackness. No one spoke, except for Dad's continual whispers of reassurance into the fear-flattened ears of his beloved horse. If we toppled overboard, it would be total loss.

Sandu knew where the opposite shore was even though it was not visible to us. He had done this many times. Exiting was easier than entering as I discovered when Sandu secured the barge to the anchor point. Everyone, including Simi, was eager to step onto terra firma.

Dad paid the boatman for the full fare at the opposite side of the river. It was not an issue of paying half then and half now. If we had been lost in the river, it would not have mattered if payment had been made in full ahead of time or not. Dad reached under the wagon seat and pulled out a small wooden crate he had specifically packed for Sandu.

"My friend," Dad said as he stepped back onto the barge platform. "Tonight, you have something extra in the bottom of your tomato box. Enjoy the taste of our house wine, courtesy of Antonia. She wanted to reward our safe travels tonight."

I think I know why my mother had done this favor. It was her son's first night ride to market. She no doubt would not sleep well.

Ahead of us were many miles of travel before daybreak. Our scary night traveling was not over. I could now see what Dad had tried to point out from the distance before we reached the river. The wall of the big forest towered in front of us, and it was blacker than I had imagined.

––––––

The forest opening was like a tunnel through the trees. When the Germans cut the paths through the forest, they cut in straight lines, several miles in length when possible, before making necessary turns to navigate to their intended destination. These series of zigzags allowed them to snake through the dense forest and drastically reduce the miles of travel. It was sad to think of why these paths were originally clear-cut. Military machinery on merciless missions had rumbled down these same paths where we now trudged through the night.

I retrieved the blanket I had been lying on and snuggled close to Dad on the wagon seat. The darkness thickened, and the night air chilled. Maybe it was my imagination, spooked by the sounds that echoed from behind the dark forest walls that arched above me, but I wrapped the blanket around my shoulders for added protection and warmth. It was darker, much darker the further we plunged into the forest.

"Are you sure the horse can see where to go?" I asked.

"He has better night vision than you and I," assured Dad.

The wagon rocked and jerked over the rougher terrain, and I was not so convinced. It was too dark for either Dad or me to see this, but I could imagine Simi's ears were pinned back and his eyes wide with fear. Simi could smell danger.

A mysterious snort startled me and spooked Simi!

Simi jammed his hooves into the forest bed, but the weight of the wagon and the slippery surface of tree leaves and twigs caused him to slide and the wagon to career on the path.

Dad pulled on the reins. "Whoa, Simi," he said as calmly as he could. Dad had braced his feet, but the last jerk in the opposite direction sent me flying forward. I lost my balance and fell. Dad swung his right arm out and caught me before I went overboard.

Dad exhaled heavily. He had been holding his breath for too long. I still held mine. The horse's breaths heaved with force into the thick night.

"All is okay." Dad spoke to the horse and me.

"What happened?" My lips quivered.

"Simi was spooked by something up ahead. I think it was a Russian boar."

"A Russian?" I hissed.

"No. It was a wild pig like the ones hunted in the woods near Vasile's home. They're sometimes called Russian boars because they're as mean as Russians." Dad laughed.

The corners of my mouth twitched in a grin, though it was too dark for Dad to notice. I was still too scared to make a sound. I wondered what other forest creatures roamed these tunnels at night. Now, I had "Russians" on my mind as well.

Dad did not think the horse was hurt. In the daylight, he knew so many things simply by looking at his beloved horse and recognizing the smallest clues, and though it was pitch black in the forest now, he knew Simi needed a rest. Dad educated me on Russian boars while we waited.

"Grandpa Cismigiu often hunted Russian boars when he was a young man," Dad began. "These animals can weigh over three hundred kilos. They're mean, very mean, and aggressive if you provoke them or they feel threatened. But Grandpa was a brave man and a good shot with his rifle."

I interrupted. "The pig we butcher at Christmastime is not mean and scary."

"You're right, but these boars look different from domestic hogs because they have to survive in the wild. They have tusks coming out of their mouths, like huge upside-down fangs. When their mouth closes, tusks are visible from their lower jaw and tuck outside their upper jaw. Anything trapped in this jaw lock has been severely punctured and will be ripped to shreds when the huge boar whips his head a few times."

"Do you really think what spooked Simi was a Russian boar?" I asked, hoping for a different answer.

"I'm pretty sure it was. I heard the snort. In the daytime, when we come back this way, you will see puddles of water on the path. This path is not protected from the rain, so runoff from the hills rushes down through here and forms large puddles. The boars like to bathe in these. During the heat of the day, they get in these water holes and root around. Some puddles are deep. A large boar was probably lingering around a water hole up ahead and we scared it as much as it scared us."

I doubted that mysterious creature was more afraid than I was.

"The boar is gone. He ran off deep in the woods, and he just wanted to snort goodbye." I could tell he tried to lighten the story, which was difficult to do on such a dark night.

Dad seemed convinced that he had let Simi rest long enough. "I'll climb down and check the harnesses to make sure nothing was twisted loose."

I tensed again. *Was it safe? What if the Russian ...* I touched my pocketknife to make sure it was still there.

In pitch-black darkness, Dad spoke softly to Simi. "Let me check your breaching. I'm going to follow it up to the crupper, to see if it's in place." I could hear his fingers rub against the leather. "Your saddle is snug and the bellyband is still attached." Dad patted the horse.

Simi knew his master's touch.

The wagon rocked as Dad adjusted the harness collar. It had rotated slightly. Simi was a muscular stallion, and he had taken the jolt quite well. Dad whispered in Simi's perked ear, and I could hear him rubbing the horse's mane.

"You're a good horse, Simi. You make me proud. We must keep going." I envisioned Dad patting him gently on the nose and then walking back to the wagon, keeping his hand on Simi's coat until he reached the step. Dad climbed back up in the wagon seat.

Not many words were spoken as the tomato-laden wagon with its two riders and horse weaved its way on through the midnight forest. It would be several hours yet before daybreak.

I was wide awake. The jostling of the wagon as it rumbled over branch and bump made for no bed of comfort anyway.

Several more times, Simi seemed to whiff boar scent lingering in the stagnant air as we passed other puddles. Each time, he lunged forward.

At daybreak, when the morning mist lifted from the earth and predawn slivers of gold glimmered in the eastern sky, the forest path emptied to a paved road heading up the mountain. It was only a short distance now to Focșani.

The rhythm of horse hooves on the pavement was melodic. The clip-clop echoed to announce our approach.

Dad did not have to look at a wristwatch. He was never late to market. He knew the importance of arriving on time. By early afternoon, it would all be over and the return trip would begin.

The mountain folk always welcomed tomatoes from the Cismigiu farm. These were so much better than those being sold by other market peddlers at booths supplied by government-run gardens. There is no comparison to the taste of a red-ripe organic tomato freshly harvested from the fertile soil of a valley farm.

It was amazing to see the marketing process in motion as people lined up for a chance to buy this treat. Well before noon, I uncrated the last tomatoes on the market table Dad had rented for the morning. Customers sadly turned away when the table was empty. If we could have brought more tomatoes, we would have sold more.

We spent the early afternoon buying goods to haul home in the wagon. We had to strap down the empty wooden tomato crates, using a few to pack in the supplies Dad had bought: corn for the horse and for grinding into cornmeal; bags of wheat for grinding flour; boxes of nails and an assortment of lumber for building shelves in the barn; pump parts and piping for irrigation; as well as gloves and bicycle inner tubes. Never the same list of items, but always a list. Neighbors and relatives also made shopping requests from time to time, and Dad always obliged.

Having managed the forest passage and river crossing without incident on the return trip, it was nearly midnight when Simi pulled us through the main gate at home.

13

White Ghost

~ Summer 1982 ~

CLOUDS dotted the night sky on one particular return trip from Focşani during early harvest season. We had gotten a late start. The blackened forest and rushing river were behind us, but we were still far from home. It was near full moon, but the clouds cast spotty shadows on the ground as the wagon rumbled on through the countryside.

I was taking a turn in the wagon seat, holding the reins. Dad had packed a few extra blankets so he could stretch out on the wagon floor to get some sleep.

A flash of white caught my eye—and was gone. It was more than a shaft of moonlight. *What was it?* I was tired but presumed I could manage the remainder of the trip without waking Dad.

And then I saw it again.

Was it a ghost?

I gasped and jumped sideways in my seat. Simi, feeling the movement of the reins, jerked in the direction he thought I was taking him. Dad rolled and bumped his head on the wagon rail. He shot upright and shouted, "What's going on?"

I turned in the driver's seat, knowing Simi would not mislead us. "Look—behind the wagon to the left," I shouted. "Do you see it?"

"Slow the wagon," Dad said.

My instinct was to slap the reins for Simi to run faster. This white shadow had spooked me, but I pulled on the reins and Simi's canter slowed to a trot.

Dad whistled and cooed, "Here boy."

It had been hanging back in the shadows, and now it came running alongside the wagon. It was an Old English Sheepdog, pure white.

"Stop the wagon!"

I reined in Simi, who seemed happy to rest, and the wagon rocked to a full stop. The dog circled in front of Simi playfully, then returned to look up at us.

His tail wagged like a flag in a windstorm. His white fur glistened in the moonlight. I fell in love with him right then and there.

"Where did you come from, ole boy?" Dad asked as if the dog might answer. "You are a long way from home. There are not many homes out this way."

The countryside we passed through was well known for grazing sheep. We often saw shepherds tending their flocks on this expanse of land. On occasion, we might see a crude mud hut used by shepherds to take refuge from a storm or the hot sun. But the area seemed deserted tonight.

Sheepdogs are protective, and those we'd encountered on prior trips became agitated when the tomato wagon rolled by the flock they had responsibility to protect. They charged, bounding across the pasture, barking warnings for us to keep our distance. There was no such thing as a friendly sheepdog when on duty. But this sheepdog looked as if it longed for attention.

"Can I get down and pet him?" I handed the reins to Dad as if he had already answered the question affirmatively.

"Be careful," Dad said as my feet hit the ground.

The white ghost had turned out to be friendly. He licked my hands and tried to lick my face. He had no collar or name tag.

"I'm afraid he might follow us home," Dad warned.

I had the same thought, but that would actually be a dream come true. I'd always wanted a big dog like this one. I rubbed the thick fluff of fur behind the dog's floppy ears.

"I wish we had something to feed it," I said.

"Good thing we don't. He needs to return home." Dad shrugged. "If we feed him, he might follow us too far."

Dad was right. Surely, a dog this beautiful had a master, somewhere. I climbed back onto the wagon, and the dog cocked his head to the side and looked puzzled. I recovered the reins from Dad and gave Simi the get-up-and-go signals.

The dog sat there. I watched his silhouette fade into the shadow of night, and then he sprang from the blackness and ran toward our wagon. This dog was not returning anywhere. He was going somewhere.

"I think he likes us," I said, hopeful he would follow us all the way home.

We rode in silence for a few minutes, the dog happily trotting beside our wagon. Dad watched him and thoughtfully concluded, "One thing I envy about the dog's life ... at least he is free to choose his master."

"If we keep him ...," I said carefully, "I would like to call him Fulga. He reminds me of a giant snowflake."

"We'll feed him when we get home," Dad said. He always showed kindness to animals, especially to orphaned ones. I took that for the "yes" answer I had hoped for.

14

Beating the Bureaucrats

~ Summer 1982 ~

I WONDERED how long someone missed the sheepdog before giving up thinking it would return. Strange, how Fulga never strayed too far from our little farm. When we continued our midnight excursions over the river and through the forests, taking tomatoes to the Focşani market in the early part of the season, Fulga never tried to come with us. He preferred the safety and comfort of the farm.

By mid-August, each picking cycle grossed three metric tons of tomatoes, and the cycle repeated itself every three to four days. With this increase, we needed a larger market.

Dad found the produce transportation policy extremely restrictive. Making a decent living to support a family of five by farming, even if conditions were favorable, was an arduous task. The system was designed with the cards stacked in the government's favor. Dad knew that to survive, he must beat the bureaucrats at their own game.

Dad sought out larger markets in areas not conducive to growing tomatoes so that a sustainable customer base would heartily welcome the quality of his offering. Unfortunately, these destinations were a long distance away and required a covert mission to transport our product to the mountainous Transylvania and Moldova regions.

Without access to markets, there were no sales. Without sales, there were no profits. Without profits, our family lifestyle, free from communist control, was in jeopardy.

We picked, packed, and prepared about seventy-five wooden crates for market each picking cycle during the heat of summer. On some occasions, it was near two in the morning before we retired to bed, only to be up at dawn to continue our duties.

We piled the crated tomatoes near the main property gate, and then Dad and a small crew of helpers—usually Marin, Pavel, and I—started another cycle of transferring the crates to the train station two and a half miles away using the horse-drawn wagon. It took three trips to get all the crates relocated, and each round-trip took seventy-five minutes on a good day.

The Siret Valley soil was rich with nutrients. I'm not sure what events during creation might have caused this, but I wondered if the seasonal overflow of the Siret and Bârlad Rivers might have attributed to it. Most cities and towns in our home region sat upon a high plateau, preventing the floodwaters from reaching the town center. But Torcești wasn't so lucky. The town center and the neighboring countryside were located in a flood plain; therefore, the train tracks did not come through Torcești. The train station was southeast of our farm in a small settlement, called Ivești, perched on a hill above the danger zone.

The horse had level ground to pull the loaded wagon most of the distance to the train station. The last half-mile was a steady incline, but the last one hundred yards, approaching the town plateau, were a challenge, as the path to the top abruptly and steeply inclined. Dad knew what his stallion could do; Simi knew what he had to do.

"Whoa," Dad said softly as they approached the base of the hill. The command was not necessary; Simi knew the drill.

All the crew climbed down and scaled the hill on foot. Dad jumped off the wagon and located a large rock, muscling it up to the wagon floorboard by his seat. He climbed back up and sat while holding the reins. Simi seemed to instinctively know what was next.

The stallion studied the path to the top, as if picking his footholds for the climb. Simi lunged forward, digging his hooves deep into the stone path and charging up the steep incline.

Rocks ripped out from under Simi's hooves, shooting down the hill and ricocheting off the wagon's wheels. All the crewmembers stood atop the hill—not in the path of these stray "bullets."

Halfway to the top, horse and wagon could strain no further. Dad jumped off and grabbed the boulder from under his wagon seat. His boots slid on the gravel as he raced back to brace the large rock behind a wagon wheel.

Simi held his position with the full weight of the tomato-laden wagon on his collar harness straining against his neck. Dad sprinted back up the hill, grabbed the bit rein, and signaled to Simi that it was okay to ease backward—thereby relieving the sheer weight of the wagon from his shoulder harness.

The horse sweated profusely, rippled muscles twitched with adrenalin, and nostrils flared to oxygenate his lungs. Simi had grit. He stood like a hardened soldier, holding his fighting position. Each ascent was a victory, satisfying the stallion instinct bred into his body. Dad rubbed Simi's nose and patted him on his thick neck.

"You're doing well, my friend. Just one more pull. Ready when you are."

Dad stepped back to the wagon, his boot heels also kicking a few rocks loose as he gripped for sure footing. Then he swung into the wagon seat and gently lifted the reins.

The horse craned his neck, looking to see if his master was in place, then lunged forward and jerked the wagon with a bolt of energy. Simi topped the hill, pausing only to allow us riders to hop back in the wagon, then continued at a strong trot. The wind in his face cooled the drops of sweat streaking his body.

15

Beating the Train

~ Summer 1982 ~

THE train was scheduled to arrive at ten a.m. Seldom was it early, but we could not afford to assume it would be late.

The stationmaster knew the approximate number of railcars on the approaching train, which gave Dad an idea of where to position the tomato crates.

The average train consisted of eight passenger cars and two parcel boxcars. Each parcel boxcar had sliding doors centered on either side for loading and unloading, a door on each end through which the adjacent railcars could be accessed, and a small office with a window. An onboard parcel attendant oversaw the delivery and pickup of inventory at each station.

It was on one of these two rear boxcars that Dad hoped there would be room for his cargo. These boxcars were not for transporting perishables, only parcels; however, everything has its price.

Dad left home with one thousand *lei* in his pocket. This was almost a month's wage for the average worker. That was a lot of money, especially to be spent on one trip to market. There were many interaction points along the transport network, and each point needed a little coaxing to keep things moving.

First, we had to secure the attention and trust of the train stationmaster. We were regular patrons at this time of year, and the stationmaster knew us well. Nevertheless, Dad needed to confirm his assistance and approval every time. A few Romanian *leis* changed hands to get this process started.

Dad paid the stationmaster for a written manifest stating the shipment contained three thousand kilos of parcels, not perishables. Other authorities or inspectors along the numerous junction points during the lengthy train ride to the Carpathian Mountains would find the tomato crates marked as "Parcels," and the bill-of-lading would usually satisfy their inquisition and allow this contraband to continue on its journey. The police and inspectors were less concerned that something forbidden was being done using the bribery system and more concerned that a paper trail covered either their willing participation or their willful ignorance of the crime.

There was always the threat of a link breaking along the supply chain. There were ridiculous schedules to be timed and met, many helpers to be hired, and authorities to be bribed. But Dad had developed a good reputation with many along the trade route. They knew he was trying to provide for his family and bring a desired commodity to others.

Dad calculated the length of the approaching train but had to guess where it might actually stop along the track. Strategic placement of the stacked wooden crates saved several precious seconds at a critical moment when every second counted.

The train was scheduled to stop for two minutes. It was always two minutes. This was not a transfer station, so the schedule only accounted for the quick unloading and loading of people and parcels. There was no delay to account for the onboarding of seventy-five tomato crates.

Dad nudged Simi to pull the wagon along the outside track, at the point where he had estimated the parcel boxcars might come to a stop. He and his crew carried the tomato crates over the track, stacking them in piles on the platform between the two sets of tracks.

Dad dispatched me to secure additional hired help that could be counted on precisely when the train arrived. There were large grain silos next to this train station that employed many laborers. I enlisted recruits from these ranks. These men knew my father was honorable and would pay them cash, and they welcomed the extra *lei*.

MARK LEE MYERS

I weaved through the grain workers, looking for familiar faces.

"Young man," a new voice whispered.

I turned to look up at the man.

"I know about your father," he said. *What does he know? Is this man a friend or foe?* He smiled with his eyes. "Can your father use an extra hand today?"

"There always seems to be too little time when the train arrives," I said. "Do you know what to do?"

"Yes. I have been told by your regular helpers."

Within minutes, I'd secured six regulars. The newcomer would be a welcome seventh. The timing of their involvement would be risky from both the standpoint of being caught by their superiors as well as not catching the narrow window of opportunity to load the cargo in less than two minutes. They would be illegally making money on the side.

Their mission required that they make a mad dash from the grain silos, cross the tracks ahead of the arriving train, and assemble on the platform by the wooden tomato crates without being seen by their bosses or run over by the train.

The horse-drawn delivery wagon returned for two more trips from the farm to the train station, and all seventy-five boxes were stacked on the station platform moments before the whistle echoed across the valley heralding the train's arrival into Iveşti. One of the hired farmhands would return the horse and wagon home when the train-loading frenzy was over.

The seven silo workers glanced at the approaching train and casually drifted in the direction of the silo boundary. The decisive moment was approaching.

Like rabbits darting from cover, seven silo workers dashed from the shadows, jumped across the web of train tracks in the serving yard, and reached the loading platform between the main tracks seconds before the locomotive screeched by, horn blasting and air brakes hissing.

We attempted two more maneuvers to guide the engineers to stop the train at the desired loading platform position. These maneuvers didn't always improve accuracy, but a few extra moments when the train stopped seemed worth the additional risk and expense to my father.

Dad stood at the highest point on top of the stacked tomato crates, waving his hat in a horizontal figure eight to signal attention from the passing engineer to where the wooden boxes were positioned on the platform in hopes of stopping the parcel boxcars at this ideal location. Any distance in front or behind would make loading harder. Every foot counted.

"Don't trip and fall," Dad yelled as I took off on my assignment. It did little to calm my nerves.

I ran the track toward the far point where Dad had estimated the locomotive would come to rest. There was seldom the luxury of time to walk the distance and await the train's arrival. In addition, there often were two trains arriving and departing the station at the same time: one northbound and one southbound.

I felt the rumble of the approaching northbound train under my feet as I attempted to outrun it. I could run faster down the middle of the tracks, hurdling the railroad ties, rather than contending with the loose ballast outside the tracks. Brakes screeched and hissed as the engine and I passed the station. I could feel its breath on my neck. I loved to run, but running for my life was completely different. I was scared. But I ran because my father needed me to do so.

The engineer leaned out and looked backward as the train rumbled to a halt. I ran to his open window and held up the fifty *lei* my father had instructed me to offer. It was too late to suggest any position adjustment of the rear parcel boxcars closer to Dad and the loading crew.

The purpose of this monetary gift was to thank the engineer for whatever effort he had attempted already, whether much or little, and to try to influence him not to pull out of the station before the tomato harvest had been loaded. The tip rarely made much difference—it bought a few moments, not minutes. I wondered if the fright and risk we took was worth it. Dad never complained. He savored every second of extra time whether real or imagined.

The scene on the platform as the railcar and boxcar doors flung open reminded me of a beehive instantly alive from a whack with a stick. Passengers exiting and passengers entering bumped into each other. Voices shouted commands and nobody seemed to listen. I zigzagged a running path through the labyrinth of people and packages, and by the time I reached the rear boxcars, I was out of breath and had a few new bumps and bruises.

The engineer had misjudged the distance. The nearest parcel boxcar lacked fifteen yards from the stack of tomato crates.

The loading platform was at ground level, much lower than the floor of the boxcar. Men hoisted and slung the tomato crates with speed and deftness, but there were more than tomato crates in motion. There were also parcel packages to load and unload in the rush. There was no time to sort out the mess. Dad and I jumped into the parcel railcar.

16

Long Ride

~ Summer 1982 ~

THE train whistle blew two minutes and thirty seconds after I had handed the "gift" to the engineer. The locomotive jolted forward, the succession of heavy-metal clanks echoing as each railcar jerked forward. The train chugged away on its northerly route.

"I love your adventurous spirit," Dad said. I knew he also welcomed my assistance. I felt proud of the work I could do even though I was only ten. My brother and sister stayed at the farm and assisted Mom with the continuous harvesting cycle and chores, but I knew this was no joy ride. Dad's elbow nudged me. "Let's get to work."

It was a huge risk to transport three thousand kilos of ripe tomatoes in boxcars only approved for parcels. Many things could go wrong along the way. Dad knew most of the parcel boxcar attendants, stationmasters, and inspectors assigned to this route. If not, a few more *lei* changing hands made for quick introductions and longtime friends.

The Iveşti stationmaster insisted we start our ride in the parcel boxcar to help organize the tomato crates strewn across the floor. It was important that parcels not be blocked so they could be quickly unloaded at the upcoming stations where the agitated beehive scene would be repeatedly played out. We stacked the tomato crates out of the doorway and arranged the parcels according to a delivery order provided by the boxcar attendant.

Our journey to Transylvanian and Moldovan mountain cities, with all the intermittent stops, took seventeen to eighteen long hours. Sometimes, we preferred to remain as ghost riders, not moving forward to passenger cars. It prevented the curious eyes of passengers and inspectors from wondering and asking where we were traveling and why. Thankfully, many of the ticket takers collecting the fares were not much interested.

"Today, let's get some rest," Dad said.

I didn't hesitate to bolt to the forward boxcar door. I loved the thrill of stepping across the open space between the two railcars, seeing the rails and railroad ties flash by underneath the train. A whoosh of air whipped around me as I stepped across to the threshold to the passenger car.

The passenger railcar had a hallway against the full length of the car on one side and subdivided passenger rooms along the other. I ran down the corridor, glancing inside passenger compartments for an available one. "This one, Dad." I motioned for him to follow as I darted inside.

It was a welcome reprieve when we did not have to share a compartment with other travelers. Each compartment had two benches facing each other: one facing forward, the other facing backward. It was an added bonus if the wooden benches were cushioned. Each compartment was heated in the winter, but lacked air-conditioning. In the sweltering summer, the windows had to be slid open to make the ride more bearable.

Every city, big or small, had a market corresponding to its size. We rotated between cities to help ensure a fresh customer base.

There were many train routes in the mountains, but this first leg of the journey always took us to a major exchange point, the city of Ciceu, close to Miercurea Ciuc. The monotony of this first twelve-hour portion of the trip was exhausting because the train stopped at every station.

We typically arrived at the Ciceu station around ten p.m. Ciceu was nestled between two mountain ranges at an elevation above

2,250 feet, very different from the forty-five feet above sea level at the Cismigiu farm. The station was alive at this late hour. Travelers scurried and zigzagged around the cargo stacked on the congested station platforms, but it was less frantic than it had been in Iveşti. This chaos was slightly more controlled.

Sharp pops and hisses echoed like gunshots up the mountain canyons as air hoses were disconnected, separating railcars from locomotive power. The distinct aroma of creosote mixed with diesel fuel and burning coal filled the night air with an industrial stink.

The extended layover at this exchange point allowed for a more organized transition. There was more time than at the previous stations, as passenger cars and parcel boxcars were swapped to various locomotives for the appropriate routes into the mountains, but there was still a lot of work to be done with the wooden crates labeled "Parcels."

We unloaded the wooden tomato crates by ourselves onto the platform, and then we hired helping hands to move the crates across the expansive station to other loading platforms near the departing train. If we were fortunate to have our cargo arrive on the boxcar destined for our city of travel, we had time to spare. But luck was rarely on our side.

Vehicles with little gas engines and small rear wagon beds carried parcels from one platform to another. Their size allowed them to fit between the train tracks and maneuver in tight places.

There was no official governing body coordinating hiring the service of those who drove these little wagons, or at least none that could be trusted. Our mission to market was illegal, and the tomato cargo was considered contraband. This made it extremely difficult to approach any official to ask for assistance.

I was amazed at the number of people Dad knew along the way. He had connections that proved valuable, especially when encouraged by incentives from his money pouch. He enlisted the service of a forklift driver to keep from handling the tomato crates twice by unloading straight from the inbound boxcar into the waiting outbound boxcar. He approached a driver directly and offered one hundred *lei*. A willing driver was never difficult to find.

"We have at least an hour before our train departs," Dad said after the "parcels" were loaded securely in the proper boxcar waiting to be connected to the outbound locomotive. "Let's get a sandwich and drink. You look tired, Son."

I had slept some in the afternoon heat as the train rolled down the tracks; nevertheless, I felt exhausted. The day had begun a long time ago. I could already sense that after many years and numerous market trips, this routine would become wearisome. My body should've been more resilient at my age. Dad, however, looked like a tough general ready to conquer the next battle.

I yawned long and hard. The night was still young.

17

Morning Market

IT was midnight when the train bound toward Bistriţa left the Ciceu station. The train moved at a slower pace due to the gradual incline deeper into the mountains. I rested my head out the open window, and the midnight air ruffled my hair and swirled inside. The air was getting cooler as the altitude increased.

The train was climbing through a tunnel of trees. Lights from the passing train windows flickered across tree branches. This reminded me of the ride to market with Dad on the horse-drawn wagon. I felt safe inside the passenger car with no threat of a wild Russian boar.

I stretched my arm out the window—it seemed like I could almost touch the tree limbs. The rhythm of the train and gentle rocking of the railcar lulled me to sleep, my head cushioned on my arm and my fingers fluttering in the breeze outside the window.

——

The train whistled like a squawking rooster, announcing arrival at Sărăţel at three a.m. There was direct, overnight train service to Bistriţa from larger cities to the west, but our approach from the southeast required that we disembark at Sărăţel for the five-mile trek to the Bistriţa market.

Dad yawned and arched his neck to stretch out a kink caused by the wooden back of the bench he had used for a pillow. He lifted his hat and combed his fingers through his hair, then tugged it back in place, straightening the brim. Not a word needed to be spoken. We both knew the drill. We both stood and were in motion before the train came to a stop.

Hurriedly, we walked down the jouncing passenger car corridor toward the rear, balancing ourselves by touching both sides of the narrow hallway. I heard rustling noises through the cracks under the doors of other compartments as some travelers also prepared to depart at this station.

We were the only ones trotting down the passage. We had more to do than most when the train stopped. This would be another two-minute stop, and there was no one awaiting our arrival; no burly men from the silo or farmhands from home. We needed to somehow unload the seventy-five wooden tomato crates in less than two minutes. We jumped down to the platform before the train jerked to a complete stop. Every second counted.

By the time we reached the rear parcel boxcars, someone had already opened the doors. Dad leapt inside like a cat. Two men stood nearby illuminated by the station lights, eagerness beaming on their faces. They had arrived early looking for work, hoping for less competition than might be found when the next train arrived closer to daybreak. With a wave of my hand, I beckoned for their help, and the two sprang into action. There was no time or need for explanation.

I climbed inside and joined Dad in shoving the tomato crates to the door opening, where the two men slid them off and stacked them in teetering towers. Any crate not unloaded in time would ride on in the night to some distant destination. I can only remember one time when it happened. Dad had shrugged it off as a gift to some needy soul when the few unclaimed crates would have been discovered in the corner of the boxcar.

None were left or lost this time, though. Dad shoved the last crate to the door opening and one of the men grabbed it. Then we jumped to the platform as the whistle blew and the train jerked into motion.

As the train pulled away, Dad observed the scrambled tower of tomato crates. It was not a pretty stack, but there had been no time to waste aligning them. The goal had been accomplished by the four of us in two minutes: all crates accounted for with no apparent tomato damage. Dad adjusted one top crate to ensure it would not fall.

"Do you men have means or desire to help transport these crates to the Bistriţa city market?" Dad asked.

"We have a truck." As one of the men spoke, the other reached for the dolly standing on the platform. They were prepared for action.

Dad bargained for a fair price, but he didn't press too hard. Five miles was a long way to haul seventy-five crates. He knew the value of help from these men and the use of their truck. Both parties felt lucky this morning.

———

Bistriţa was a typical Transylvania city, carved from the landscape and weathered by time. It was clean and colorful. The Bistriţa River etched the eastern edge and tree-topped hills, and distant mountains rimmed the horizon.

The Romanian culture was seasoned over centuries to enjoy good food with good friends, so even though there was less to celebrate under communist rule, the hunger for normalcy remained. Food quantity and quality were no longer a common luxury, and the search for both drove the city market to be bustling.

There were grocery stores, but these were not the modern-day mega-stores where stock clerks labored around the clock to keep items arranged on shelves for shoppers. A delivery truck arrived once per day, normally between five and six a.m., and the line of customers started forming around four, long before the front doors opened. There was always a plentiful supply of canned items, but perishable meat and dairy products were the coveted commodities.

Meat was butchered to order but not to selection. A patron might request a cut of meat, a roast or a steak, but the butcher would instead slice off the next portion; the patron was given the selection that he saw fit to cut and package. A person could take it or leave it, but customers took it without complaint.

Dairy products were dispensed in a similar fashion. They were rationed until gone. And they were always gone before all orders could be filled.

Grocery stores did not offer perishable produce. Produce was subject to spoilage, emitting unpleasant odors. This was especially true with the poor-quality produce mass-produced on government farms where the best specimens were exported. Therefore, the tradition and necessity of regular visits to open-air markets in search of better quality and variety was a way of life.

The Bistriţa city market had a typical layout: rows and rows of tables, some covered, some not, primarily for fruits and vegetables, no livestock. The booth manager was stationed near the center, where government-set prices for each commodity were displayed on a large board.

––––––

One could set a clock by Dad's arrival to market. There was much to do, and time was precious trying to get ready for when the market opened with customers who were ready to buy.

We first had to settle a tax with the market manager. The tax was calculated by weight rather than by number of crates, typically around two hundred *lei* for the entire load.

We rented a scale, as it was too much trouble to bring one from home. There was no time to be worrying about a scale when all hands needed to be free and available to load and unload the tomato crates from the railcar. The rented scale was an equal-arm balance type. An aluminum three-gallon bucket hung from one side arm and iron weights from the other.

It was important to get a covered booth at the beginning of a row to be more visible. Dad always paid extra for this advantage and rented two tables instead of one. He rented the booth all year long and when he was not there, the booth manager knew others were welcome to use it. It did not matter to Dad if the manager double-rented it to someone else on the days we were not there. That was not Dad's concern. Dad wanted to make sure he would have the advantage of first choice when he showed up.

Dad was not the only one selling tomatoes, but his would be the best due to the soil they were grown in and the care taken to pick, pack, and ship.

We stacked the tomato crates neatly in rows behind the two tables under the booth covering to protect them from the sun, and we tilted three crates with open lids facing forward on one table, displaying their contents. We placed another open crate and the scales on top of the second table. We were ready for business.

"Remember, always appear active and ready. Never sit down on the job," Dad said.

Dad and I knew our plan. It was a script we'd rehearsed in preparation for this day at market. It was not a matter of *if* it would be necessary to save us from serious consequences from the police, but a matter of *when*.

———

The line had grown to more than forty-five people waiting their turn to buy our tomatoes.

The man standing in position seventeen from the front looked no different than most. If I had been told there was a member of President Ceaușescu's secret police, the Securitate, somewhere embedded in the line, I could not have readily picked him out of the crowd.

He was dressed in rural clothing, his weathered cotton pants torn in a few places from apparent hard work. His shirt was soiled to match the appearance of his trousers. His shoes were thick-soled, unpolished, dusty-black. He could have passed for any factory worker just getting off a night shift and stopping by the market to buy food on his walk home.

His face had the five-o'clock shadow from yesterday's unshaven whiskers. If one looked closely, only his hands seemed out of character. They were too clean, with no dirt under the fingernails—the pristine look found on one who sat behind a desk.

There was another thing a person might notice by studying those standing in line. The faces of many were forlorn. Their eyes stared blankly at the back of the person standing in front of them or off into space at some distant focal point. They were accustomed to standing in long lines to purchase necessities.

In contrast, customer number seventeen was alert. He was not staring at anything or anyone except me. He was observing every transaction.

The line inched forward. I was selecting, weighing, bagging, and selling tomatoes as fast as a ten-year-old boy could. This was a lot of responsibility. Money and tomatoes changed hands from buyer to seller at a steady pace.

Number seventeen advanced to number two. The intensity of his observation was evident now to anyone who might have been watching, but I was focused on the current customer. I selected one more tomato and placed it on the scale. The weight tipped slightly over three kilos.

"Three kilos," I confirmed looking up into the customer's eyes. "Is that what you wanted?" My father had taught me to make sure the weight on the scale was always tipped in the customer's favor.

For the first time, maybe in a long time, the customer smiled and said, "Yes ... thank you."

The little handwritten sign lying on our table read "3.00 *lei* / kilo." The official price board hoisted in the center of the market stated that tomatoes were only one *leu* per kilo, one-third of our price. That was the price set by the government to discourage competition.

A profit could not be made selling at that price unless farmers and peasants working for peanuts grew the tomatoes on government-confiscated property. The Cismigiu tomatoes were organic, and the effort and time it took to transport them this far demanded a higher selling price.

The locals were thrilled for the opportunity to buy our tomatoes. The average Romanian living under Ceaușescu communism had a decent monthly income subsidized by a government handout to try to keep citizens content. They had money but limited products to buy. When news spread about an available product, people stood in long lines for the opportunity to advance to the front before the supply ran out.

MARK LEE MYERS

Rarely did I need to say the total cost aloud. The asking price was listed on the discreet handwritten sign lying on the table. Most customers handed me the correct amount of money based on the weight they purchased without being prompted.

The mystery man advanced to the table and asked me for one kilo of tomatoes. This was an unusually small amount based on the wait time in line. People were desperate to buy, so most customers bought extra either for themselves or for their friends and neighbors. People helped each other so not everyone had to stand in every line every day. It was common for one customer to buy seven kilos. Sometimes five or six purchases would empty one tomato crate.

"Just one kilo?" I asked to confirm.

The man nodded. I picked up two tomatoes, careful not to break their skins, and placed them on the scale. My father's tomatoes were vine ripe, meaty, and larger than any others found elsewhere. The two tomatoes tipped the scale at slightly over one kilo.

The man laid one *leu* on the table and reached for the bag into which I had placed the tomatoes. I was confused and did not immediately realize what was happening. I had gotten into the rhythm of selling tomatoes and was acting on autopilot.

"It will be three *lei*," I said. When I glanced up into the man's eyes, I recognized the look. His eyes were narrowed, and he had a slight grin twisted at the corner of his mouth.

"Do you know who I am?" the man asked, narrowing his eyes.

I snapped alert. I felt scared, more than I had dreamt I would be if this ever happened, but I played my part very well. I had practiced this in my mind so many times. I showed no alarm or emotion.

"No, I have never met you."

He ignored my comment and continued without answering his own question. "The market price for tomatoes is one *leu* per kilo."

Dad sensed the line flow had changed. He was watching from a distance, which was part of the plan.

The man raised his voice and started making a scene.

"Where is your father, young man?"

Dad came running. "What is going on here?" Dad asked, playing his part.

"You are in violation of government policy," the man said, scowling and turning to face my father. "Why are you selling tomatoes at a higher price?"

"I don't know what you are talking about." Dad actually knew very well that the government intended to force his compliance, and if he were found not obeying, they would take him to jail, not just fine him. A violation was considered a felony—and arrests happened all the time.

Dad had purposefully stayed away from the booth, nowhere to be seen, but secretly observed with a close eye and ear from a distance. I was his excuse and escape route. He had put me in what appeared to be full charge of the selling operation.

This man, glaring and demanding answers, was a member of the secret police. His job was to check for overpriced products and make examples out of people who violated policy.

The agreement between Dad and me was that if this ever happened, he would rush back to the booth acting surprised and appearing to sharply reprimand me. He needed to make it look and sound as if he was unaware of my selling tactics.

"What did you do!" demanded my father, turning his attention to me. "What is this?"

Dad snatched up the handwritten sign lying on the table. I had purposely written it in my own childish scrawl.

"I did not know there was a set price," I said, cowering in false shame.

Dad apologized profusely to the police officer and tore the paper sign in half. I was a minor and the police could not do anything to me. Dad was dodging a bullet.

The policeman barked a reprimand. "You need to know the market rules!"

I stood there looking glum, eyes lowered, with my hands tucked in my pockets. I hoped my practiced look of innocence was convincing. Dad glared at me, playing his part in mock frustration, and the police officer looked askance, darting his eyes between the two of us.

The officer yelled, "Don't let me catch you charging more than the posted amount for your tomatoes again!" He then did an about-face with an air of superiority and marched off, clutching his one-kilo bag of tomatoes.

It would not be the last altercation, but luckily, the same police officer never caught us again. We sold tomatoes in several mountain cities and rarely returned to the same city two weeks in a row.

The government wanted to bankrupt farmers like my father, betting they would give up and quit. But they underestimated my father. He was not a quitter. He was a survivor.

From the market opening at six a.m., we worked hard and usually sold all seventy-five boxes before close. But at times during the season when competition was stronger, it might take two days. On those occasions, we often slept at the market because the booth we rented was covered. The night's rest was not comfortable but adequate. Sometimes a person living nearby invited us to spend the night in a real bed, and Dad always accepted and paid the rent.

When the crates were empty, Dad again hired the men with the truck to help reverse the process back to the train station. We flung the empty crates into the parcel boxcar with time to spare within the two-minute rush when the train arrived. On a good trip, we were back home in Torceşti on the third day.

———

The harvest at home required picking every three to four days, so life was constantly busy. Mom was better than Dad at organizing and coordinating, so she managed the farm while Dad embarked on these extended selling excursions. The warm sun had continued to ripen tomatoes and the harvesting crew had picked and packed the next batch while we were gone, so the cycle of marketing madness for Dad and me started over at daybreak the next morning.

18

Seeding the Future

~ Summer 1982 ~

DAD started his tomato business by purchasing smuggled Belgian seeds. There was not enough seed locally available for purchase. Smuggling was a necessary form of commerce. Communist policies and practices did not prevent it, though; inadvertently they encouraged it.

"Why would they limit the amount of seed sold," I asked.

"Communism has a warped definition of the marketing law of supply and demand; they limit supply in order to have more control. It is all about retaining power by suppression of liberty and any entrepreneurial drive," Dad said.

Long before communism had curtailed and controlled what was printed, my father read an article that mentioned new and improved methods of manipulating production for higher yields using chemicals. This didn't sound natural, because it wasn't natural.

Nature was wonderfully created to regenerate, with no need for man to meddle with the formula. My father learned from Grandpa that now was not the time to start meddling. He hoped his children and grandchildren for many generations would also carry on this God-given tradition.

The illegally imported seeds gave my father the start he dreamed of, but he needed to discover a more economical and sustainable way to replenish his seed supply.

Dad planted the Belgian tomato seeds and produced a great harvest that first year. From then on, he collected seeds from each year's crop and augmented them with a small portion of imported seeds until production could sustain his desired quantity.

Seed harvesting was so vital to sustaining good crops that Dad chose to do this task himself. But he felt it was time to teach me his tricks.

His collection process was simple. He walked through the field looking for the best plants with the best tomatoes. He then painted a line on those plants so the harvesting crew would know to leave those tomatoes for his picking. He took pride in his hand-selected specimens, taking them to the preparation area he had set up beside his compost pile.

"Start by helping your mother bring the jars to the table near the barn," Dad said.

Mom and I lined numerous clean glass jars on the surgical table, where Dad carefully dissected and extracted the valuable seeds. He sliced each tomato in half and gently squeezed each section over a jar, filling each one about half full with tomato seeds and juice. He tossed the empty tomato skins onto the compost pile.

"Okay, let's carry these jars into the barn," he said. Dad grasped two jars, one in each palm, but I knew to only take one and secure my hold with two hands. I searched for tripping hazards as I followed him. Dad placed the jars on shelves out of direct sunlight.

The seed mixture developed a whitish mold on the surface in about five days. Dad showed me how to scrape it off before adding water to fill the jars.

"Gently swirl the liquid mixture, and the good seeds will sink to the bottom," Dad said. My first attempt was too harsh.

"Just do it slowly." Dad tipped the jar, pouring off the floating seeds and pulp. "We will repeat the process until the seeds are clean."

Dad then poured the clean seeds out onto a fine mesh-covered frame, which allowed for further draining of moisture before the seeds were sprinkled onto drying trays and left for another three days.

We stirred the seeds at least twice a day until they dried thoroughly to prevent them from sticking together.

Finally, we transferred the seeds to dry, airtight jars and stored them in the cellar. Another generation preserved. And hopefully, another bountiful harvest.

19

Chewing Gum & Cap Guns

~ Summer 1982 ~

THE pain started in my lower back.

"It's probably just a muscle spasm," Dad told me. This was reasonable, given that I had hoisted and toted hundreds of tomato crates all summer long. No one suspected a herniated disk, which was discovered many years later in my adult life. The warning signs were there, but we didn't know what to look for. As the summer progressed, we knew it wasn't normal for a ten-year-old to limp and drag his foot.

"We need to get you treated," Mom said. I could hear both concern and urgency in her voice. She then outlined my new adventure.

Lucky for me, Dad's brother, Uncle Ionica, lived near a resort town, Băile Felix, which catered to tourists seeking the health benefits from the area's natural mineral water and all the practitioners offering health-related services. The unlucky part was that Băile Felix was located on the opposite side of Romania near the Hungarian border.

Băile Felix was lavishly built and decorated to entice foreign travelers. The town had several luxury hotels and resorts. Romanian citizens were allowed to visit and vacation there, but they were relegated to separate accommodations—nice but not extravagant like those catering to the foreign guests.

Most of the foreign tourists were Hungarian. Hungarians were one of the largest ethnic groups in Romania, and they seemed at more liberty to travel to and from their native country. Our government may have relaxed travel requirements in order to encourage the influx of foreign capital.

At the end of summer, I journeyed alone by train to the far northwest region of Romania to visit Uncle Ionica. I disembarked after the eight-hour train ride at the large metropolis of Oradea, where I boarded a bus to travel to Haieu, the suburb where my uncle lived.

Băile Felix was a short walk away from the Haieu bus station— even shorter if I walked a mile through a field connecting the two towns. The field was government-seized property, set aside for public use. With their property confiscated, livestock owners needed places to graze their animals. Grazing rights on strips of land like that particular rolling field could be rented from the government. I had no need for grazing rights, nor was I interested in paying a toll. I simply enjoyed the shortcut.

Folks in Băile Felix were thoroughly impressed with "The Moldavian" from the other side of the country. They were amazed I had not been intimidated riding the train all the way across the country, alone. Little did they know that I was a frequent train traveler, helping my father transport tomato crates to distant destinations. I did not share the reasoning for my courageousness. I let their imaginations run wild with suppositions and conclusions that elevated my bravery and prolonged my celebrity status.

My physical therapy to stimulate circulation and relieve muscle pain, stiffness, and spasms included mineral water baths, massages, and paraffin hot wax treatments. I was surprised to find that several of the skilled masseuses and masseurs were blind. These blind practitioners were extremely adept, focusing intently to feel their way to their patient's muscular maladies.

After repeated yearly visits, I developed friendships that got me invited into the luxury resorts for my massage treatments. Doormen turned a blind eye, probably seeing no rationale for stopping to confirm the residency credentials of someone my age. I didn't have to pay the foreigner's price. I got a sympathy discount.

It was like a paid vacation for me. And the jaunts to Băile Felix exposed me to standards of living not pervasive throughout most other parts of Romania. I felt like I was in a different country.

Foreign tourists would bring hard-to-find products from their homelands to sell or leave as tips. I remember the first time I saw a clickable ballpoint pen. Its shell advertised "Toyota," and I couldn't care less what that product might be, but I horded several pens to give as gifts when I returned home.

My adventurous spirit was kindled, and the winds of time flamed a burning desire and taste for travel to foreign soil. And then my uncle introduced me to chewing gum.

Oh, my goodness.

The flavor was exotic—a taste of freedom. The chewing sensation was magical. I chewed long after the last drop of sweetness had squirted my taste buds. I chewed until my jaws ached.

I didn't like the discomfort of lower back pain that brought me to seek relief in this faraway, fairytale place. If it weren't for the fact that my uncle also visited our family in Torceşti almost every Christmas, bringing gifts from afar, I might have sought to come back more often. I thought of him as a second Santa Claus.

One Christmas, my uncle brought me a foreign gift that sparked an imagination firestorm that lasted many years—a holstered, double-pistoled toy. The cap guns simulated gunshots when the hammer struck a percussion cap encased on a red paper roll. The realism was accentuated with a puff of smoke that allowed me to raise the pistol barrel to my lips and blow the "bullet" vapor into the wind, just like a real gunslinger. With the toy guns, I was the coolest kid in town—the one and only cowboy. With holster on my hips, I even walked with a cowboy swagger.

20

Bonding

~ Fall 1982 ~

THERE were two good reasons to celebrate—school started September 15 and my birthday followed three days later.

The start of school was the beginning of the end of tomato harvesting for the year. The magnitude of manual labor and the relentless schedule of survival were wearisome, so a change of pace in autumn—and the winter holiday season that followed—was a welcome relief.

Farming was not just a home chore, so the total work reprieve was not immediate. The government enlisted middle-school students, from fifth to eighth grade, as part-time farmers. For the first three weeks of school, the government had a "volunteer" program for middle-school children to work in farm fields, helping with harvests of corn, grapes, and ... yes, tomatoes.

The government controlled thousands of acres of farmland scattered across the fertile Siret River Valley. The leaders tried incessantly to propagate the "everybody is equal" philosophy, and this school work program was no doubt meant to indoctrinate a feeling of indebtedness to others and instill national pride. But in reality, free-labor was probably the main motivator for its conception.

Here we go again, I thought as we lined up to board the vehicles. The government arranged for students to be picked up in small cars and buses and driven to a nearby government-controlled farm.

Kids earned about ten *bani* per bucket picked, so it was not an absolute volunteer program. Part of me liked the brief diversion from school and the extra money, which added up to about one hundred *lei* per season, but it reminded me a little too much of our family business.

The innocence of youth may have shielded me from the realities of our precarious life—trying to live free of communist containment—but I had deeper discernment than I gave myself credit for at the age of eleven. I wasn't thinking so much in terms of what I was missing in comparison to others around me in my own country, let alone how children might be privileged in foreign countries. I was living with the cards I was dealt.

The adventures and tests of 1982 were foundational for life's experiences that awaited me in subsequent years. Even today, I approach many opportunities and challenges with the perspectives ingrained during those formative years.

I began fifth grade and a new school at the same time. There was no school bus pickup at my home. In fact, there weren't any school buses at all.

Classrooms for fifth to eighth graders were located three miles away, past the train station in Iveşti. I had three options for transport: walk, run, or ride my bicycle.

I chose to peddle my way to and from school, and there were challenges riding in both directions. The road was gravel most of the way, which made for a more strenuous workout. The last incline right before town where Simi struggled to pull the loaded tomato wagon was no easier on two wheels. I often walked my bicycle to the top.

The return trip in the wintertime was after dark as class was conducted in the afternoon and the sun set early. After descending the hill, the road stretched for at least a lonely mile with no homes in sight, only open fields on either side.

I was spooked by the memory of stories Grandma had told of real wolves that roamed the area not many years past. Now, every wolf-sized bush in the shadows frightened me. I may not have ever admitted it to anyone, but the three-mile trek home was a white-knuckle ride, not just because the loose gravel required a tight handlebar grip but because my nerves were on edge as I imagined all sorts of dangers.

Dad was kind enough to harness Simi to the sled and take me to or retrieve me from school when the roads were impassable on my bike due to snow cover. But the chill of the winter wind or the rain in a storm was no excuse to escape school. I don't remember school ever being cancelled due to inclement weather.

I have fond memories of homework, as strange as that may sound. I can't remember much of what I studied. It was the family time that was special.

The communist agenda to conserve energy was not because of an environmentally green movement; government officials were more concerned about paying off national debt than they were about their citizens' comfort. Frequently, the electricity was shut off around eight p.m. and did not return until long after I went to bed. But this had the effect of drawing families together.

Late evening found us children huddled around a candle to catch the light flickering from its flame in order to finish homework assignments, with Mom sitting nearby crocheting and Dad dozing in a chair. Peaceful.

The earlier portion of the year had been a whirlwind of activities that afforded little time, if any, for bonding. Now, we giggled at the shadow puppets we made with our contorted hands and fingers in front of the candlelight, casting reflections on the wall. These were our homemade cartoons.

When the cold winds blew outside and the snow began to fall, our home was cozy with the radiant heat from our wood-burning stove. We were fascinated by the fire's magical properties as we flung orange peels into the flames, enjoying the aroma and the sparkle and crackle that resulted.

These were memories in the making.

21

Winter White

~ Winter 1982 ~

LET it snow, let it snow, let it snow. That was the greatest wish I had in the wintertime.

I must have had Eskimo blood running through my veins when I was young. So did all the other kids in my hometown. We were oblivious to the cold. Misery is inconceivable when a child owns a sled.

Almost every kid I knew had some sort of sled. Many were homemade from iron tubing, cut and welded into a platform.

The toboggan-style sled Dad bought me was made for export out of the country. Made from pressurized wood, it allowed the front to curl skyward with a metal plate on the bottom. It looked very cool. And as its owner, so did I.

I don't know what it cost him or what the return favor might have been to obtain this prized possession, but I was the envy of the town.

December arrived with a little bit of snow here and there, but when Christmas school vacation started on the fifteenth, every kid in the county was bored silly if there was not a full blanket of snow on the ground.

There was no dedicated weather channel on television to predict weather patterns. In fact, there were no TV programs at all to get excited about.

Not only was the television signal bad, but the content was nothing but propaganda spewing for two hours each morning. I always wondered who would take time to sit and listen to it. And then there was nothing broadcast for almost ten hours. The TV displayed white noise until six p.m. It looked like a snowstorm. Then at six p.m., more government propaganda blared for another hour followed by fifteen minutes of cartoons. The whole of children's entertainment was from seven to seven-fifteen p.m. After that "excessive" amount of time, more government propaganda and communist ideology streamed across the TV until ten p.m., at which time the TV went into "snowstorm" mode again until the next morning.

There was little to do inside in an era before video games, smartphones, or electronic entertainment. Children opted to play outside.

———

Mom was the first person out of bed in the mornings, even before Dad, and even on the coldest of mornings. She stoked the wood stove and added wood chips, leaving the stove doors open, which allowed maximum heat to radiate outward. We woke up during the winter to the comfort of a fire because of Mom's selflessness.

Mom had time in winter to cook things that filled our home with aromas of love. One such memory was the smell of warm cheese pastries in the morning. I love to cook because my mother showed me how to bake these treats. She made the dough from scratch, rolled it out, and layered it with fresh, homemade cheese. The warm, flaky crust she pulled from the oven at daybreak smelled and tasted heavenly.

I awoke listening for the scrape of a snow shovel, the clue that a significant amount of snow had fallen overnight. Before leaving the warmth of my bed, I could hear that wonderful sound of Dad shoveling paths to the front gate, to the woodpile, to the water source, and to the barn. One my age hoped for at least a foot of new white powder.

Nothing got me out of bed faster, even on a cold morning. I darted to the window to see Dad wrapped in a heavy coat and hat with snow still falling and collecting on his clothing.

If it were a weekend or during the holiday break from school, Mom would not bother fixing a big breakfast on a morning with fresh snow. She knew we kids would scurry outside, wasting a good portion of a hot meal. There were ten to fifteen kids living on our road, and many more in Torceşti. We were all outside from morning to night when the ground was covered with winter white.

The noise level echoing across the river valley was strong enough to trigger an avalanche if there had been any mountain peaks nearby. Instead, the roar of voices rumbled over the farmland, filling the valley with a chorus of excitement and laughter.

The best spot for sledding was a short walk from our home to a hill overlooking the Bârlad River. This was a collection point between our home and the kids living in town. Nearly one hundred kids romped in the snow together on a white winter day. The downhill slope swept toward the frozen river, and the competition was to see who could go the farthest on their sled.

I positioned my sled at the crest of the hill. I felt all eyes were on me as I sat down and dug my fingers into the snow to hold the sled in place. I glanced to my right and left. Other kids were lined up—ready to race—but no one was making a move to challenge me.

I effortlessly pushed backward to cock my arms in place, ensuring I had a firm grip on the crusted snow bank—and then I yanked forward, uncoiling my arms behind me as I thrust off the cliff. I leaned back and stretched out to reduce wind resistance and heard the whisk of wood slats gliding over the packed snow. My sled was better at staying on top of the snow because it was a long toboggan design. The sleds made from welded iron tubing produced more friction and dug into the snow.

My sled picked up speed. I felt the rush of air across my cheeks and whisk of snow under the wooden slats. At the bottom of the hill, the force of gravity shifted as the ground leveled, and I thought I'd glide forever. I coasted beyond the compressed snowpack and powder puffed as my sled settled into its softness.

Cheers of onlookers erupted, whooping down the slope to congratulate me on setting a new distance record.

We also played hockey on the frozen river. We did not have ice skates, but we were equipped with a creative array of hockey sticks, carved from tree limbs and lumber. A leather shoe heel served well as a hockey puck.

My mother, certainly not unlike so many others in the community, worried about the dangers on the ice. It was not only the worry of the injuries caused by the lack of protective hockey gear but the fear of the ice being too thin.

The dangers of a situation are not part of the calculation in a child's mind. The formula for fun is commonly measured in proportion to the amount of activity, adventure, and challenges from childhood friends. The river's ice seemed thick enough to a child my age, but the current was constantly flowing underneath the surface.

We ventured south to where the Bârlad riverbanks were tree-lined, forming a tunnel. This was a beautiful place where we loved to congregate and play. The evergreen trees and hardwood trunks contrasted with the serenity of white snow, but the protection we found from the wind also altered the water temperature.

We often went to the point where the pylons of an old German bridge jutted up through the ice partway out from the riverbank. The water ran deeper in this part of the river, which also meant the water underneath was warmer and the ice thinner. That was an irresistible invitation—a challenge—to see who could get closest to the edge of the ice midstream where the water was free flowing, unfrozen.

The toboggan design distributed my weight over a longer area, which meant I could dare to reach closer to the unsafe edge. Lying on my belly, face-forward on my sled, I used my gloved hands to inch out a greater distance than anyone else dared to go.

"Go farther!" several boys goaded.

The others held their breath.

MARK LEE MYERS

I knew I was probably too close to the free-flowing water where the ice was thin, but the awe-stricken admiration from my playmates bolstered my courage and numbed my nerves. Falling into the river at this point either might sweep me under the surrounding ice or cause hypothermia before I could make the distance back home, soaking wet.

The ice snapped, cracked, and popped. I turned to retreat, twisting to swing the toboggan under me and shoving with my boot. I remember the sting of the frigid ice water as my leg busted through. I clung to the sled and kicked frantically. The ice was now fracturing beneath me with every forward thrust. A brave onlooker rushed toward me, grabbed the front of the sled, and gave a tug that pulled me back to safety.

I caught the eyes of my siblings staring from the sidelines. I could not tell if their expressions were of admiration or admonition. I swore them both to secrecy. They understood the consequences of our mother finding out.

An inner voice told me to be thankful I was still alive and cautioned me to never do it again. I would be lying if I said that was my last time.

At noon, Mom had lunch ready, but we were reluctant to come in. We feared being denied the chance to return outside in the afternoon. Our clothes were damp and frozen, so Mom forced us to stand around the wood-burning stove. This seemed most unnecessary and a waste of our playtime. We begged for leniency on her house rules, but she wouldn't give in to our whining until our clothes were sufficiently dry.

———

The best time to play outside was at night under a full moon. The reflection off the snow's crust made it look like daytime.

Kids tied dogs to sleds to pull them across the snow, and Fulga's bear-size paws whisked me around effortlessly. My dog's name meant "Snowflake." He was a large ball of white fur.

Harness bells rang holiday tunes as horse-drawn sleighs passed along the snow-covered roads. We waited for a wagon to pass by, and then we ran behind and grabbed hold to catch a free ride crouched on our sleds. We sometimes created a chain of twenty sleds in length. On a good run, we might be pulled for a half-mile before letting go and walking back.

We played outside until whistles and hollers from parents beckoned us home. We prayed for the snow to not melt overnight and for more to fall before morning to replenish what we had trampled that day.

Snow covered many imperfections, and merriness covered misery.

22

Slaughter

~ Winter 1982 ~

TOILS of the year were now frozen in the past. Many families had experienced hardships, but we had endured additional difficulties due to our father's resistance. The winter holiday season gave promise to enjoy time and traditions.

In the days leading up to the Christmas holiday, families focused on hospitality and festivities to bring a bit of normality and to end the year on a positive note. In those memorable times, we lived from moment to moment, savoring the change of pace that lifted our spirits.

Citizens forfeited a portion of their dignity, unless they were members of the ruling regime assigned to micro-manage society. Those who had embraced communism for self-preservation also were subject to the shortages of goods to purchase and restrictions on activity and travel abroad. Along with their assets, they had also given up their freedom.

In our home region of Romanian Moldova, it was a common Christmas and New Year holiday tradition to slaughter a pig to supply fresh meat and trimmings for the festivities and to provide sustenance into the coming year with sausage, ham, and bacon. Many families butchered their pig on December 20 to celebrate Saint Ignatius' Day, but the exact day at our home varied from year to year. It was always done before Christmas.

The slaughter started before sunrise, and it often felt like the coldest day of the year, so the adults drank shots of *pálinka* to warm themselves. The vintage was the current year. I assumed *pálinka* tasted best when consumed fresh because there was never any remaining come the following fruit season.

Dad's distillery looked crude, but it was effective. He inserted a cauldron into a small brick furnace sized to allow only for a few pieces of wood at a time. A hot fire would have scorched the brandy. The vapor from the fermenting plums escaped from the cauldron and passed through a spiraling pipe submerged in a barrel of cold water. The vapor condensed into a liquid and collected as it dripped from the end of the pipe. The fragrance in the air was a mixture of pungent alcohol and arid, smoked leather of smoldering wood.

There were many tasks of preparation and execution of the pig slaughter and, thankfully, many helping hands to accomplish them. Relatives and friends congregated at our home. Everyone knew their role without anyone dictating orders. It amazed me how many people were involved and everything ran smoothly. These simple-life citizens who the government scorned as peasants were very capable of managing their own affairs. They were the true lifeblood of the societal fabric—resourceful, responsible, and respectful.

While men set up tables outside and sharpened carving knives and cleavers, women boiled large quantities of water and arranged bowls and spices on tables inside. Wherever the squeal of the pig was heard, kids could be found.

Dad lured the fattened pig into a corner pocket he built in the pen, then he grabbed the back legs, tied them together, and pulled the pig out. The pig started squealing. We heard other pig shrills echo over the countryside from similar slaughters by our neighbors all morning long.

Four or five of us wrestled the pig and held him down on top of a fresh bed of straw piled thick on the snow. This is where the pig slaughter commenced.

Dad loved animals and was kindhearted, but he believed our food supply was God-given and our Creator intended for meat to be a food source. Dad conducted the slaughter with respect and efficiency.

I had watched him many years now as he laid the razor-sharp blade against the pig's skin and slit its throat, causing quick death by blood loss from the jugular vein and carotid artery.

I had matured quickly from the experiences of life during the past year. My self-confidence at eleven was at a new high. I was helping hold down the pig when Dad asked if I wanted to slit the throat this time. I was honored, and I was nervous. I had always thought about doing it someday, but he had caught me by surprise.

Many eyes were watching, and I wondered if the other boys were envious, but my anxiety came from a feeling deep inside—not wanting to disappoint my father. Dad handed me his knife, and I made a swift, clean cut, precisely as he had always done. I could feel Dad's pride and see it in his eyes. He nodded with approval.

We lifted the pig into a metal trough, drenching it with boiling water to clean it and remove the hairs. Men hoisted the carcass by its rear feet until its head dangled above the straw-covered snow. We cut off its head and carried it into the house in a large bowl, where women carved out delicacies of meat. We gutted the pig, making an incision the full length of its abdomen, cut the body in half to allow better cleaning, and left it to hang in the cold air to make the deboning easier.

Men carved out the various cuts of meat, transferring the chunks to indoor tables, where women trimmed and sliced it into respective hams, chops, bacon slabs, and sausage scraps. Little was wasted.

It smelled like a butcher shop as women rubbed prepared seasoning and curing salts on select cuts, churned meat scraps through a sausage press, and flavored hams in a smoker. Most of the meat was packaged for the freezer, and some the women started cooking. The aroma of sour vegetable soup broth made with savory pork meatballs permeated the house and drifted outside each time the door was opened.

It was a feast from the pig, nothing fancy. But to me it was a special taste and a special day.

Some relatives stayed overnight and helped finish the process, and the old folks—anyone not desiring to play in the snow—continued the feasting and celebration. More eating, more drinking, more storytelling. I might have learned more by staying to listen to their tales, but I figured there would be time enough for that later in life. I darted out the door and into the night with cold air pricking my face, leaving snow tracks as I ran to find my friends.

23

Perfect Christmas Tree

~ Winter 1982 ~

PINE trees were scarce in the Siret River Valley. It was not a picture-perfect bucolic setting where we could hitch up the horse and wagon and ride out into the woods to cut down the tree of choice. I remember the anxiety of purchasing a Christmas tree.

Dad woke at three a.m. two days before Christmas, which meant Mom had slipped out of bed a few minutes prior to stoke the woodstove and make him a warm drink. The barn at this time of day was its coldest, and Simi uttered a soft nicker as he recognized Dad approaching his stall in the darkness. There was no need to waste fuel by lighting a lantern or switching on a flashlight and consuming battery power. Dad could hitch up Simi with his eyes closed, and they might as well have been closed now; it was that dark inside the barn.

The ride to the Iveşti train station should've taken less time than when Simi pulled heavy loads of crated tomatoes, but the weather was bitter cold, so Dad allowed the horse to trot at a slower pace. This helped both horse and rider brace against the frigid air.

Arriving at the train station, Dad hitched Simi to the horse rail, draped a blanket over him, and tipped the stationmaster a small amount to watch and care for the horse during the next six hours. Dad rode the next train north; his destination was Tecuci, about one hour away.

He arrived at Tecuci before sunrise and hurried to the marketplace to claim his place in the long line. The line was sure to lengthen by one hundred people before sunrise.

The frozen figures stood with their backs to the icy wind, talking to those in the line near them. When the truck arrived with Christmas trees cut from the Carpathian Mountains and the cargo hastily unloaded, the formality of the line eroded into a frenzied rush. There was no time for contemplating the selection. Customers grabbed the first tree their hands could reach. There were always fewer trees than customers.

There were two years I remember that Dad left Tecuci empty-handed, but he found an alternative before arriving home. The alternative was branches snapped off hardwoods and tied together to resemble a tree.

Mom woke up my brother, sister, and me for breakfast at about eight a.m. on the morning Dad went to buy a Christmas tree. Breakfast warmed our bellies, but our excitement was already on fire.

We listened with one ear tuned to the road for the sleigh bells signaling our dad's arrival. At the first sound of distant jingling, we pressed our noses against the front window, straining to see him coming. Then without coats, hats, or gloves, we darted from the front door and met him at the front gate.

We were never disappointed in his selection. Every tree was magical. Each had its own asymmetrical natural beauty and filled the house with a sweet scent of pine so intense that it tingled my sinuses.

We erected the tree in the living room and waited to decorate it until after we had eaten supper on Christmas Eve. We improvised a tree stand by filling a five-gallon bucket with cornmeal and wrapping the bucket with decorative foil. We trimmed the tree the same way each year. An unlit star graced the top, and a strand of twenty bell-shaped, blinking lights looped around the branches. Snow clung to the tips of twigs and pine needles in the form of flakes we had pulled from cotton balls. Fifteen glass globes, vibrant with colors and glitter, reflected the joyous atmosphere as they shimmered below branches where they hung. Candy chews, wrapped in assorted-color foil twisted at both ends, dangled from strands of thread.

We wanted to preserve the magic and ambiance of the tree, and we discovered that the candy wrappers could be untwisted at the bottom to release the sugared contents and then re-twisted and puffed to appear intact. By the time we disposed of the tree after the January 6 holiday to celebrate the baptism of Jesus, called Boboteaza, it had not lost its beauty nor had we forgotten its significance. The star still shined, the bells still glowed, the cotton-snow had not melted, and the ornamental globes still sparkled ... but all the foil candy wrappers hung empty.

24

Holiday Happiness

~ Winter 1982 ~

THERE were many religious traditions around the Christmas and New Year holidays, but the Communist regime imposed restrictions, especially in the larger cities. We enjoyed more liberty to celebrate traditions in our rural area.

The fun and festivities began on the morning of Christmas Eve and commemorated one of the most important winter customs: going from house to house wishing everyone happy holidays and blessings for the New Year by singing carols.

There were two different caroling celebrations. The first, called *Colindul,* commenced on the morning of Christmas Eve. There were three separate performances: the first conducted by the young boys on Christmas Eve morning, the second by the teenaged and unmarried young men on Christmas Eve night, and the third by the parents on Christmas night.

The preparations started at least a week in advance, especially for the non-adults. Small groups of friends met and chose a selection of traditional songs and practiced their performance skit in the days leading up to showtime.

This caroling tradition was executed slightly differently in the various regions of Romania. In the Moldova region where we lived, the young boys woke up before daybreak and met at a predetermined point on the edge of Torceşti, and then proceeded to walk from house to house. Not every home, of course, but we planned a good route that took us to those we felt were more likely to gift us better with the typical sweets, cakes, and money.

Even though people might still be asleep, we opened their gates, went up next to their windows with small bells in hand, and started singing carols. There were a variety of responses, mostly favorable, being that we were part of the first wave of singers.

Some people were generous, some less so. Relatives gave the most. Word traveled fast to the other groups of kids following a similar footpath, so the homes where occupants were freer with their gift giving had kids lining up in the street waiting their turn to go forward and sing their rendition. My father's tomato business was more lucrative than a typical government job at a factory or Communist-controlled farming operation, so my parents were able to hand out generous caroling gifts.

We loved it. We were excited more about the handouts than the religious significance. There was no competition, but we met other groups of kids on the streets of town and compared our accumulated stash, which often totaled around two hundred *lei* plus the sweet treats.

The tradition for generations past only had been for the older teenagers and unmarried men to carol on Christmas Eve, but somewhere along the line, those in my preteen age group realized they were missing out on free goodies. We were afraid to go out in the nighttime hours with the older boys for fear they would steal our gifts, especially our money. Thank goodness for the brave youngster who expanded the tradition to include this early morning prelude. It was well worth the effort.

————

The first thing on my mind on Christmas morning was: *Did it snow?!* The best gift was fresh snow on Christmas Day.

It amazed me how our parents were able to buy and hide our Christmas gifts without our knowledge. I never worried about not having a gift, and I never assumed there would be one either. It was always a wonderful surprise.

A vibrant bag of oranges caught my attention under the tree, and I snatched one, lifting it to my nose and inhaling deeply. Oranges were imported only for the Christmas holiday season, and to this day, no matter what time of year I peel an orange, even in the heat of summer, its aroma transports me back to the wintery holiday.

I also spotted one bunch of green bananas next to the oranges. These must have been imported on the same shipment because they were available only at this time of year as well.

We never could buy bananas in quantity, so Dad and Mom allowed us kids to share the few. They were always green—never ripe.

We stashed the bananas in a dark place under the bed and checked on them every five or six hours in hopes they had ripened. By the second or third day, our patience had worn thin, and we begged Mom to allow us to eat them. Hard, bland. We never learned our lesson.

———

I grabbed my coat, jumped into my boots, and quietly opened the front door so as not to wake anyone. I stepped outside, leaving footprints in the fresh snow. I was heading nowhere in particular. I wanted to experience the wonder of winter on Christmas Day.

I lay down and fashioned a snow angel, looking up and grinning at the cumulus cloud floating above. Its shape reminded me of a white dog.

We had a stealthy no-name barn cat and a lazy dog, Rex, on the farm, but they were not interested in relationships. The dog in the sky smiling down on me reminded me of Fulga. I had snuck out so quietly he had not heard me. I whistled—and my very own ball of white fur came bouncing around the corner and landed in my lap.

"Hey, ole boy. How you doing?" I snuggled him and rolled in the snow. "You love the snow as much as I do."

I rubbed his head and released him. Fulga shook his fur and hundreds of snow crystals showered my face.

Wood-burning aromas blended in the frosted air: toasted apple, oak, and pine. One lone chimney puffing smoke a half-mile away could be detectable in the wind, and almost every home in our small town had fireplaces and stoves stoked with firewood that dispersed a potent sweet smokiness over the entire countryside.

By the time I went back inside, Mom was busy in the kitchen. The savor of vanilla and rum met me at the door. Mom was baking pastries. She had rolled bread dough, cut with an upside-down cup, deep-fried to a golden brown, and sprinkled with sugar while still hot. Irresistible.

I wish the two weeks of the holidays could be frozen to last longer. This was a magical time of year with unforgettable savors, sights, and sounds.

The second caroling ritual began on New Year's Eve. It was called *Plugusorul*. In the same fashion as *Colindul*, the younger boys went from home to home in the morning, and the older boys went in the evening. On rare occasions, girls might participate, but this was a rowdy ritual more suited to rambunctious boys.

Plugusorul means "a small plow," and in Romanian folklore and the poems sung during this ritual, the plow symbolizes the hope for the bounty of a New Year harvest. This ritual made more sense to me as my father was a farmer, and the horse and plow described in these carols reminded me of the springtime and autumn plowing he did with Simi.

We sang well-wishes for a good harvest and the protection of crops. I sang these carols heartily because my family would need all the help and blessings we could get, and it helped me forget about the Communists for a while.

We thought of ourselves as plowmen as we sang these carols. We used a friction drum, called *buhai*, to mimic the moaning of an ox. We snapped a whip in the air to mimic a farmer driving the oxen, and we jingled bells to represent an oxen harness.

Part of the fun was building these stage props. We made the friction drum from a five-gallon cylinder covered by sheepskin on one end. We removed the bucket bottom and stretched the tanned sheepskin tightly over the top. We punctured a small hole in the middle of the sheepskin, inserted a hank of horsehair, about the diameter of my finger, and fastened it on the underside to a block of wood.

We held the drum between our knees or had a friend hold it for us, and as we alternated pulling on the horsehairs with wet hands in a rhythmic motion; the vibrations of the horsehairs on the sheepskin resonated through the cylinder, producing a moaning sound.

We made the twelve- to sixteen-foot-long whip from fibers of a hemp plant. We made the bell prop from small cowbells attached to a leather strap.

With the whip snapping overhead, the drum moaning its low growl, the shaken bells tingling, and the choir reciting a traditional poem in high-pitched adolescent voices, it was no wonder that so many people gave us money instead of sweet treats. I now realize they were probably paying us to leave.

The caroling voices skipped merrily across the snow-crusted contours of the surrounding countryside and the streets of Torceşti. I loved hearing the blend of carols; sometimes I could hear more than one group singing at the same time from different homes. The music in the air revived a life that was suffocating under communist rule. A new year was dawning, and the festive spirit of the holiday season renewed our spirit to live, love, and pursue liberty.

Many local gypsies also participated in these caroling traditions. The gypsies loved the flair of traditional dress and were graced with beautiful singing voices. Like the rest of us, they preferred monetary gifts to the treats.

The tradition concluded on New Year's Eve. On New Year's morning, some kids went around again in hopes of cashing in on a good idea, but Dad never allowed us to participate. By now, the patience and tolerance of the town residents had worn thin.

———

The Communists attempted to appear inspiring and generous on New Year's Eve. It was the only time something of interest appeared on TV.

TVs were a luxury, and because our family had one years before most in the community, many friends and neighbors packed into our home to celebrate the arrival of the New Year.

The TV program started with musical entertainment at about nine p.m. and lasted until midnight, when fireworks lit up the screen, blasting from some distant city, most likely the rooftop of the Presidential Palace in Bucharest. We had the TV on to enjoy the musical interlude, but no one was inside watching when the clock struck midnight.

Dad bought small fireworks, often nothing more than sparklers. I remember the reflection of the sparkler glow as it danced off the snow and highlighted the smiles on everyone's faces.

I wanted to stay up all night long; it was part of the ritual. I took a short nap in the late afternoon, hoping it would help me last until morning. Sweets and pastries filled the kitchen table, and I consumed my portion and then some, all through the night, which helped sustain my energy.

The glow of sunrise was just beginning to sparkle above the eastern horizon when my eyelids succumbed to gravity and my sugar high wore off. I crawled into bed feeling more refreshed inwardly than my body evidenced outwardly.

Overall, it had been a good year. We had persevered and survived. And the holiday season had once again given hope and happiness.

––––––

Over the next three years, Marin advanced through high school, Lenuța blossomed to her sweet sixteen beauty, and I burst through several sizes of shirts, pants, and shoes. Dad and Mom also aged, although I didn't recognize the signs of fatigue on Dad's face until it caught me by surprise.

25

Tested

~ Spring 1986 ~

THE police targeted my siblings and me, as part of their harassment plan waged against our father, by restricting our educational opportunities.

Our parents desired, as all loving parents do, that their children be educated and prepared for life's successes and challenges. Mother took the lead to seek out higher-education opportunities to influence our career perspectives beyond the farming horizon. She never explained her true motives, but, coincidentally, she chose an aeronautical technology school, as if to lift us from the soil and aim us for the sky.

High schools in Romania during this era followed a certain curriculum. While they all had similar core classes, one high school centered on the arts and literature, and another focused on technology and science.

The communist education structure didn't normally let children from one county go to school in another unless the desired curriculum was not offered within the county of family residence. To discourage this practice, the application process was cumbersome and fraught with deliberate delays.

Mother was patient and persistent. She gained approval for us to attend the highly regarded aeronautical technology high school located in Bacău, some eighty miles from home. Bacău had a military airport and manufacturing plant where fighter jets were made, hence the existence of an aeronautical technology school.

Every student completed a milestone exam at the end of eighth grade, called the *Testarea Națională* (National Test). Exam scores determined each student's future education path. The National Test was similar to what some countries call the Standardized Aptitude Test (SAT), Secondary Leaving Exam, or Maturity Exam. A second test, administered at the end of tenth grade, determined if students could continue their education, and then a final test for admission into a university was required near time of graduation.

Admission to the aeronautical technology school required a high score in mathematics and physics. Students only got one opportunity to take the National Test, so one could not afford to leave it to chance. Tutoring was common, for the students desiring to excel.

Mother knew a professor living in a small town four train stations away who could help students prepare for the National Test. He tutored my sister and brother, and then it was my turn.

We never worked in the tomato field on Sunday, but during the year prior to high school, Sunday afternoon found me baptized in textbooks. "No nap for Nicolae," I used to whine.

I rode a bicycle two and a half miles to Ivești. A friend of our family lived in the fourth house from the train station, so we had an agreement for me to leave my bicycle at his home. Without knocking on the house door, I parked my bicycle in his yard and ran to the train station. Four train stops later, I jumped from the train and walked to the professor's home for two long hours of tutoring, and then retraced my steps and rode back home.

That Sunday ritual lasted my entire eighth-grade year, and I kept each appointment come sun, rain, or snow—my mother's order. The tutoring was expensive, but she knew the importance of a passing grade. It was tough, but it taught me tenacity.

––––––

Immediately after my eighth-grade school year ended, and before the tomato harvest began in earnest in mid-July, Mom arranged for me to travel by train to Bacău and meet up with my brother before he returned home for the summer. The purpose was for specialized tutoring.

The Sunday-afternoon tutor near home was a generalist and prepared me with a broad overview of syllabus subjects, but Mom also hired a specialized tutor in Bacău, a professor affiliated with the aeronautical technology high school. He had helped my brother and sister prepare for and pass the extremely difficult *Testarea Națională*.

The test was not specific to a region or individual school. The professor was not privy to the exact questions on the exam, but he focused my attention on the necessary topics.

I'm sure Mom expected my brother to be my guardian angel on this first trip to the big city. My brother had lived in Bacău for several years during the school season and had lost his fear, being fully acclimated to city life, so his idea of indoctrination for me was a simple "sink-or-swim" method.

My brother took me across the city to the tutor's home, pointed out where to go, what intersections to cross, where to find the bus, how to pay a bus fare, where and how to transfer from one bus to another, and the various twists and turns of walking the last distance to the tutor's front door. He showed me the way there. He expected me to find my way back to his apartment on my own. I was only fourteen years old and more petrified than excited.

I was an emotional wreck. This was the biggest exam of my life. I had prepared all year with the help of the Sunday-afternoon tutor, but this was an intensified cram course, in a new big city with funny-tasting, smelly water.

I don't recall learning anything on my first day with the specialized tutor, as emotions fogged my brain, but I do remember the smells of the city as I retraced my footsteps to my brother's apartment. Trash chutes hung down the sides of buildings and emptied into dumpsters, producing ripe-rotten stench that tumbled out from the alleys as I passed each opening.

I had doubts, many doubts, that this city life was for me, but I didn't have a choice in the matter, other than to buckle down and focus on my studies.

———

I followed the footsteps of my siblings, scoring high on the *Testarea Naționalǎ*. That meant I, too, took the technology route. Relieved, I was pleased with my grade, but more pleased to have not disappointed my parents after all the tutoring. Dad had paid for it, and Mom had insisted on it. It was great to have made good on that portion of their investment.

My brother and sister came home from high school in Bacǎu for the summer to help in the tomato business. I would join them in Bacǎu after this harvest season in September, but as a young teen, I was not truly prepared for living away from home.

Mom made a huge celebration for my rite of passage into high school. I was celebrating the exam storm season being over. But another cloud was developing on the horizon.

26

Warning Signs

~ Summer 1986 ~

THIS harvest season started as most others, and my brother and I had no idea that our summer was about to change for the worse.

I was fourteen years old and feeling more mature than my age, as probably most teenagers do. It had been four years since I started my "master's in marketing" by accompanying my father on sales journeys by horse and train. By the time I graduated high school, I would already have my marketing "doctorate."

Much of my life occurred in cyclical fashion each year, but a universal truth is that time goes faster the older we get. Springtime came too soon after harvest season ended in the fall—too little time for fun and recreation, too much time for work.

Mid-July was the start of harvest season, and while I looked forward to the break from schoolwork, which was increasingly difficult and demanding, I was young enough to wish for the prospect of summer fun. Instead, most of our summer fun-in-the-sun came in the form of chores relating to the tomato field.

Dad was still in control of each trip to market. He was the wheel hub that kept things rolling and the hand-on-the-helm that steadied the progress. We had never taken the time to document everything that had to be done for a successful trip. I watched and learned through the "School of Experience." The major exam to assess my knowledge was about to begin.

———

Dad and I arrived at the Vatra Dornei train station, the mountain city we frequented most for marketing our tomatoes. The outdoor market at the center of the city was nestled right by the bridge over the Dorna River, a half-mile from where the tributary converges with the Bistrița River. The clear, cold water rushes for fifty-four miles, at the edge of roadway 17B, crisscrossing from one side to the other under narrow bridges, until it cascades into Lacul Bicaz.

The Vatra Dornei countryside was most conducive to bovine farming and forestry, so the organically grown Cismigiu tomatoes were heartily welcomed when we first arrived, and the demand never waned. Where there is need, there is demand, and where there is demand, one can more easily find accomplices willing to help rather than hinder.

Dad had developed many relationships here, and there was less competition from other sellers. The relationship benefits included everything from transporting our product to and from the train station to helping protect our higher-than-the-government's market produce price by alerting us to the whereabouts of the secret police who frowned upon the practice.

The market manager at Vatra Dornei became our friend and worked to preserve and protect our repeat appearance. He often mediated bribes to the police before they could cause us trouble. This required a supply of tomato crates full of tomatoes stashed in his office.

The secret police were everywhere. Though often unseen, their repressive presence could be felt. Many loyal customers helped identify the undercover police, tipping us at appropriate times to temporarily alter our selling price to comply with government pricing regulations and prevent arrest. These mountain people desired to help because they understood the economics of what it took to provide Siret River Valley tomatoes to their remote locale.

———

I saw my first squirrel in Vatra Dornei. There is a large park, called Parcul Central, neighboring the back of the market. After our final tomato sale of the day, when Dad canvassed the city to purchase supplies, I got to run in the park and chase squirrels. I bought nuts and tried to feed them, too. I never got a squirrel to trust me enough to eat out of my hand, but I always left my gift piled in the park, and it was never there when I returned.

My romp in the park must have worked as a sedative, because my eyelids lowered when the sun set behind the hilltops each time we pulled away from the city and headed home.

I often dreamt about this mountain city, lush and green with one-hundred-foot Scots Pines trimming the hilltops. I often wished we could come back in the winter when snow decorated this landscape, but we never had the luxury of a wintertime excursion to this northern region of Romania.

———

The day was progressing normally, and we had a steady flow of customers, but I noticed Dad sitting down more than usual.

I assumed Dad was delegating more to me, so I didn't think much of it at first. He did not normally wear his feelings on his face because he had a high pain tolerance, but I noticed the look in his eyes and cadence of his walk were different.

Dad watched our booth from a distance, alert for trouble from the secret police, and I never gave much thought to where he was. But today, I was more alert to his whereabouts. I caught myself unconsciously watching him.

Out of the corner of my eye, I saw Dad stumble and fall, rolling instinctively to keep from busting his kneecap. I dashed from the booth so quickly I startled my customers, but I knew their eyes followed where I was running.

Dad grasped his leg with both hands. I dropped to his side but felt helpless. I gripped his shoulder and braced his forearm.

"A sharp pain." He spoke through clenched teeth. "My leg gave out on me."

"What should I do?" I asked.

"I'll be okay." His breathing was labored. "I'll be okay."

I was not convinced.

I looked up to find a ring of people towering above us with expressions of curiosity and concern. I felt like we were on an operating table with surgeons glaring down at the gurney. I assumed most of our customers were still standing in line, awaiting my return to the sales table. They could help themselves as far as I was concerned.

Dad sat up too fast. His eyes rolled, and his head wobbled. He was fainting.

"I'll get some water," someone said and sprinted off.

I helped Dad lie back down, and I rubbed his forehead and cheeks. He felt clammy. He opened his eyes and looked into mine.

"Lie still," I instructed. "Someone has gone to get water. What else can I do?"

"Serve the customers." I was not surprised he said that.

"Don't worry about the customers, Dad. They can serve themselves. I am staying right here until we figure out what's going on."

I felt his body relax a little, but I could sense the pain persisted. His leg was still tense.

"Something hasn't felt right all morning. How many crates are left?" His mind was still on business. It was useless to avoid his questions. Maybe talking about the tomatoes would take his mind off his pain.

The person who had sprinted away returned with a pail of water and a rag. "Do you want a drink first, Mr. Cismigiu?"

I looked at the man for the first time. I was surprised he knew our family name, but then I recognized him as a regular customer. We had been coming here for two years, so it was no surprise he knew more about us than we knew about him. I felt bad. He was just another customer to me. We obviously meant something more to him.

Our customers were loyal. It was amazing that even when there were other farmers in the same market selling tomatoes on the same day, our booth had more customers in line patiently waiting their turn to buy.

Our tomatoes were the best. This was a fact. Dad did not allow a bad-looking tomato to be packed into the wooden crates. His quality control started long before the tomatoes entered the packing department in our barn and continued to the moment of sale. I knew of no other farmer who cleaned each tomato by hand with a damp cloth prior to crating.

I believe the popularity of our booth also had something to do with my age. Customers liked the novelty of a kid like me conducting sales transactions with a smile.

I was no doctor, but my analytical brain must have developed by this age. I tried to make sense of what had just happened. This was more than a leg pain. Dad looked pale. His skin reflected an inner malady, and his countenance was too passive.

My mind raced.

We were too far from home.

Dad looked exhausted, the strain on his face disquieting. He had always had the strength and stamina of an ox. I couldn't recall him ever visiting the doctor, let alone a hospital. There was a toughness in his body armor that always seemed impenetrable. We both had confidence in his abilities for the same reasons, which is why we both felt rattled by this new vulnerability.

I helped him sit up again and drink a little water. I dipped the cloth, wrung it out, and wiped his forehead and cheeks. I was surprised he let me do it. He inhaled slowly and deeply, tilting his head backward until his lungs filled, and then he exhaled faster until his chin rested on his chest. I dipped and wrung the cloth again, laying it across the back of his neck.

Several onlookers dispersed, but the water-pail man knelt at Dad's opposite shoulder.

"I can help walk you back to the booth," he offered. "Your booth is covered. There is more shade."

Dad lifted his head and smiled with his eyes. "That would be good."

With both of us tucking one hand in Dad's armpit and another braced under his elbow, we raised him to a standing position. His steps toward the booth were cautious and calculated. We served mostly for balance. I sensed all eyes followed our slow movements, and most activity around us stopped as we passed by.

Dad settled on top of a tomato crate. As our helper walked back to retrieve the water pail, market activities returned to normal. I started serving customers again.

"May I have the pleasure of knowing your name?" Dad asked when the man returned and placed the water pail beside him.

"My name is Petru." The man didn't offer more information, but he hesitated as if it would be okay to ask.

"Hello, Petru. Close friends call me Cuţa. I remember seeing you many times before. Thank you for being a faithful customer."

"Thank you for growing excellent tomatoes. We appreciate the effort it takes for you to bring your product to our market. I heard you are from the Siret River Valley."

"Yes, we are. We live outside Torceşti."

"I've heard it's beautiful there," Petru said. "How do you feel, Cuţa?"

"My head is not so foggy, but my leg still feels weak. What is your occupation?"

Listening to the conversation, I focused more on Dad than the mechanics of my tomato sales. Here again, I was not surprised Dad had turned the attention to someone else and away from his own pain. He was genuinely interested in the struggles and pursuits of others.

I contemplated the "foggy head" reference. It wasn't just a leg pain after all. Dad must have felt lightheaded before his leg buckled.

"I'm a lumberjack," Petru answered.

That explained his weathered look and windswept hair. His skin was tanned and healthy looking. Forestry was a major industry in these north woods, a source of construction lumber and Christmas trees.

"I love the woods myself," commented Dad. "I help the forest warden in our home county every chance I get. It is my excuse to walk in the woods."

There was a lull in their conversation. It seemed their shared interest allowed them to understand each other at a different level and converse without words.

I swung my focus back to my customers, trying to give each one my full attention. I did not want to seem rushed and rude, but I was intent on finishing as quickly as possible.

We made it a practice that when we had ten or so boxes remaining to sell, and we were running close on time to meet a train schedule, we started offering a discount if customers bought more. I made the executive decision to enact that sales strategy now.

The train departed southbound at the same time each day, once in the morning and once in the evening, so finishing early would be no real advantage today, but I felt an urgency I could not quell. A weight of responsibility had shifted to my shoulders. The summer solstice had passed a few weeks prior, and I felt another turning point had now altered the course of this particular summer season in a way I was not fully prepared to grasp.

I turned to Petru. "Would you mind staying here with my father while I try to find Moş Hozac?"

"Moş who?"

"Oh, I'm sorry. He's the old man you often see with a horse and wagon for hire. He mumbles when he talks, so we don't know how to pronounce his real name. We just call him 'Moş Hozac.'"

I meant no disrespect, but his name sounded as scary as he looked. The Romanian word *moş* means old man. It seemed both fitting and respectful.

Dad raised his eyebrows. "Are you done already?"

"Yes. I have three crates of tomatoes remaining, and I plan to drop off two at the market manager's office and offer the last one to Petru, if he can help us out a little longer this afternoon."

"I would be glad to help," replied Petru. "You don't need to pay me."

"Then consider it a gift. I appreciate you helping when my father fell, and I would rather ensure he does not try to get up and walk around or start stacking empty crates.

"If Moş Hozac is not around the market now, I need to run out to his home at the edge of the city. I'd rather he come earlier than normal with his horse and wagon. I want to get positioned at the train station with time to spare, find a place where my father can lie down and rest, and be prepared to get our empty crates on the train with your help. The train only stops for a few minutes."

Dad was speechless. His instinct was to say that he could help, as if nothing was wrong, but he held his tongue. He later told me he was proud and impressed I had taken action and felt responsibility for making decisions given his incapacitated state.

I found Moş Hozac, Petru was well worth his tomato crate, and the market manager did not refuse the two I gave him. My instinct told me the investment in these three men might be a good insurance policy to secure their continued assistance on future visits to Vatra Dornei.

On the return train ride home, Dad remained quiet. He was a practical man, so I knew he was contemplating the next course of action to keep the business running. I was sure his thoughts were similar to mine. *What if his ailments were serious? What if he could not make the next trip to market?*

I wondered if I should have called the game warden, who had a telephone at his home, to have him relay a message to my mother. But unfortunately, I had not thought of it before leaving Vatra Dornei. I convinced myself it was better to keep her from worrying.

The train ride passed slowly, probably because I spent less time sleeping and more time thinking.

It took no arguing with Dad upon our arrival in Iveşti for him to sit with the empty crates at the train station and allow me to run home and return with the horse and wagon. He confessed that his leg was still too painful and weak to bear much weight.

It had not been easy for him to exit the passenger car on his own, but I jumped off before the train came to a complete stop and ran back to the parcel boxcar and unloaded the tomato crates. The crates were empty, but I had had no one to hand them to me on the platform. I hadn't wanted to damage them by pitching them off, but it was time-consuming jumping in and out of the boxcar. I had no choice but to let the crates tumble to the ground. The train was already in forward motion by the time I jumped to the platform.

———

Mom saw me running down the road and ran to meet me as I approached home. She knew something was wrong. We talked as we walked, and by the time we reached the barn, I had given her the highlights of what had happened.

Marin helped me hitch the horse to the wagon, and then we all climbed on board, including Lenuța, and raced back to the train station. Even Simi sensed the urgency.

Dad was sitting on an empty tomato crate when we arrived. The long train ride home with the usual transfer at the Ciceu exchange station had taken an additional toll on his body. He raised his palm and tried to hide his pain behind the facade of a half-grin.

Mom rolled up his pant cuff to examine his leg. It was swollen twice its normal size from his knee to ankle. Mom insisted we take him directly to the doctor, and Dad only dared say once, "I will be okay," because it was obvious Mom's decision was final.

My brother and I lifted Dad into the wagon, and he lay down on a bed of blankets Mom had brought from home. With tomato crates strapped down and all family members on board, Marin took the reins, and we raced toward our hometown.

The doctor confirmed the swelling was internal and not related to an insect bite or puncture wound. We feared the blockage was a blood clot. Dad's blood pressure was elevated, and a blood test indicated potential pulmonary embolism byproducts.

"You need a pulmonary angiogram," the doctor said, "but we don't have the equipment or skills to administer the catheterization in this clinic. You should see a doctor in a larger city."

"Is it really that serious?" asked Dad.

The bombshell shook us when the doctor mentioned "amputation." He inserted the word "potential" before it, but that word dissolved in midair, and we only heard and felt the gravity of the "A" word.

Dad made the next decision. This time, his word was final. He insisted we take him home and hire a nurse to come as needed to monitor his condition.

I slept past breakfast the following morning, even though the family had allowed Dad and me to go to bed immediately after supper. My parents and my brother were seated at the kitchen table when I came in search of something to satisfy my hunger pangs. My sister must have been outside doing a chore.

"You and Nicolae are the logical choice," Dad said to Marin. I didn't have to second-guess the topic. I knew another shipment of tomatoes was ready for transport.

"Nicolae is very familiar with the process, and he knows the contacts we have established there." Dad was referring to Vatra Dornei.

"Nicolae was the man-in-charge when I collapsed." Dad turned to me. "I am proud of you, Nicolae." I blushed, pleased.

I didn't know how things were for other kids my age, but I knew my experience was giving me an unparalleled education.

I felt good that my father had confidence in my abilities, and I looked to my brother, who was eighteen at the time, as my safety net in time of need as we traveled together. At times, I felt overconfident, but I had no illusions that I was still two months away from my fifteenth birthday and was taking on adult responsibilities.

MARK LEE MYERS

27

Heavier Load

~ Summer 1986 ~

DAD reviewed the plan with Marin and me. We'd make Vatra Dornei the exclusive market destination for the rest of this summer while Dad recuperated. Our contacts there were invaluable. As long as no significant competition surfaced, the tourist city and surrounding population would be a good customer base.

My brother and I started out the next morning. Nothing seemed too different, except that Dad did not participate in the bustle. With assistance from our hired help, we transported the tomato crates to the Iveşti train station in the same way we always had done. Simi obeyed Marin that morning with the same respect he did our dad, climbing the steep incline and accepting every challenge. The usual loading crew from the grain silo risked life and limb once again, and we got off to a good start without any left-behind tomato crates on the loading platform.

The first hour was busy as usual sorting the parcel boxcar and making order of its contents per the delivery manifest provided by the parcel attendant. It was not until we moved forward to a passenger car and relaxed that I started feeling apprehensive. At this point on prior journeys, my father had borne the weight of responsibility I now felt. He had done it for so long that autopilot seemed to guide him.

My mind raced at full throttle, analyzing every station we would pass through, every checkpoint we might encounter, and the timing of unloading and reloading at the exchange station. I worried that I might oversleep—if I could sleep. And once we got to Vatra Dornei in the predawn darkness, who would walk—in the dark—to find Moş Hozac and summon him out of bed to help us transport our tomato crates from the train station platform to the farmer's market?

I had the sales part perfected, but now it would also be my responsibility to manage and safeguard the profits. I tried to remember faces of those my father knew along the way—and why he knew them— and what service they provided, or what bribe they required.

Marin sat quietly staring out the train window. *What was he thinking?* Either he was not apprehensive about anything, or he was trying not to burden me with his own concerns. At each interval and intersect, he hesitated to see what I might do first. A normal teenager might be puffed up with pride if his older brother paid him this level of attention and respect, but my stature felt humbling. Our mission was not a game.

We arrived at Vatra Dornei on schedule. We were lucky to have a helping hand who sprang into action when the parcel doors opened, and I jumped inside and started shoving tomato crates to the opening. I didn't know our helper's name, but I did remember seeing him there on many early morning arrivals. He most likely had another job during the day but made himself available around the train station at this early hour in hopes of making a little extra income. I tipped him the same generous amount as I had watched my father do. He thanked me and commented that he assumed Marin was my brother, as we looked alike. I smiled and nodded. Thankfully, he did not ask about our missing father.

"Will the old man be waiting for us at the train station?" Marin asked. I knew the answer. I had avoided thinking about it for as long as possible.

Dad and I had met Moş Hozac—the old man with a white horse—in the train station on our first trip to Vatra Dornei. And that was somewhat by accident, as there were not many people in the station between three and four a.m. The old man had come to help someone else who had requested his early morning services.

He often was seen in the market area during the day, offering his services for sale, but he was not an early riser by nature. He took a liking to my father, as most folks did, and he agreed to help us any time of day or night. The trick was finding him, and at three-thirty in the morning, he would most likely be at home in bed.

I wished I could tell Marin how to find him. But I'd have to walk alone in the dark and leave Marin with the crates at the train station. This was one of the scariest things I remember doing.

The surrounding terrain was mountainous, so I walked through the city, past the market, and up a hill, winding my way along a path dotted with occasional houses and barking dogs to find where the old man lived.

The dogs there were not lap dogs. They were monster dogs, willing and ready to defend their territory from bears, wolves, and other wild animals that roamed the nearby mountains. The barking echoed up the slope, announcing my presence. I didn't want to be considered intruder or prey.

At least I didn't have to worry about my brother jumping out from the shadows to scare me. Marin was a jokester. Dad would scold us for being rowdy at the supper table and demand we step outside for a while. If it was dark outside, Marin would dart out the door, hide, and then jump out to spook me. There were spooks in the dark, tonight. I could sense them. For once, I wished for Marin to jump out.

I stopped at the old man's front gate. The darkness was heavy. I called his name, hoping my voice would reach his window without me having to venture up to his front door. He was too deaf to hear much of anything, and I was too timid to make enough noise for fear of awakening others—or any nearby creatures in the night.

The hairs on my neck stood up when I pushed the creaking gate open. I darted for the house. In the nighttime shadows, it looked shorter than he was tall. I felt safer being closer to the structure, but I feared waking the man who slept inside.

I rapped on the bedroom window, but he didn't stir. I knocked harder, shouting his name.

I heard him grunt and grumble, like a bear awoken from hibernation. It seemed to take him a while to realize what was happening. Once I heard him shuffle out of bed, I gingerly approached the front door and braced myself for the moment it would open. When it did, his hulking frame loomed in the darkness.

There were no pleasantries exchanged; in fact, his speech was still gruff as he mumbled his recognition of who I was and why I was there. He did not invite me inside, and I would have declined anyway, but he said he would meet me in the barn. When he closed the door, I did not move. I waited to venture away until he exited a rear door and turned on a barn light, illuminating the path for me to run.

Moş Hozac and his aged horse were the oldest living creatures I knew. Both were white-haired and ghostly.

Harnessing his horse was a slow process. The trek back to the train station would've been faster if I had walked, but I stuck around and tried to assist the old man for fear that if I left, he might either fall back asleep or forget where to go. But that scenario was unlikely—Moş Hozac liked the money he made helping us. We paid him one hundred *lei*—two days' salary for a few hours of work.

The old man's trailer was a big platform on wheels, no rails. His horse was boney and sluggish. I didn't think the horse could run, even if forced. Moş Hozac only worked in one speed as well. He was slow, but he was sure. Our need was great, so our patience had to be also.

———

By the time we got the tomato crates transferred and our market booth open for business, the shadows had shortened far past the opening time on the clock. I did not share this detail with Dad when he asked for our trip report. The good news I did report was that customers were lined up and eager to buy at the opening bell.

Dad had instructed Marin to perform the surveillance from the sidelines; he was to watch for the secret police and be ready to swoop in like an eagle defending its nest should any disturbance occur.

Gross sales each trip exceeded nine thousand *lei*. This was equivalent to seven months' salary for an unskilled laborer. The importance was the buying power, not the amount per se.

So what does a fourteen-year-old boy do with thousands of *lei* in his pocket at an open-air market? He worries, frets, and makes frequent trips to the bank. We had never experienced trouble in this city, but this time I felt more vulnerable. It was not the common criminal I feared, but the police I didn't trust.

Since I'd turned fourteen last September, I was eligible to get an Identification Number, used for banking transactions, so my brother and I both were authorized to make deposits as needed. Vatra Dornei had only one depository—CEC Bank—government run and sanctioned. The bank teller recognized me as the son of the tomato farmer, so it didn't seem strange that I was making repeated deposits on my own. Things weren't as computer-automated at this time, so I was simply converting cash into a certificate of deposit.

The experience of that season would be a major reason why I was never afraid of independence and entrepreneurial endeavors. I learned to drive for success long before I ever learned to drive a vehicle.

––––––

The forays to market with my brother continued the remainder of the season. I had traveled to market week after week, month after month, year after year, so the physical aspects of this particular summer job were nothing new, but the mental stress of responsibility weighed heavily on me. Considering I was fourteen, a person might think my energy level would have been fully charged, but I was exhausted.

The blockage in Dad's leg dissolved, but the family's concern regarding his health did not. His stamina diminished, but his steadfastness remained. He would continue to live free from communist fetters.

28

Home Away From Home

~ Fall 1986 ~

THE big city life of Bacău was a major culture shock to my brother, sister, and me when we lived away from home attending high school.

Cities like this one were the only place foreign products could be found for sale in stores. Items such as color TVs, stereos, and jeans were sold at a store called Consignatie, but these stores were not for commoners. Patrons had to have an issued Access Card or foreign currency to gain membership. All I could do was window-shop.

My brother was the first of our family to attend the aeronautical technology high school in Bacău. We had relatives living there, so he stayed with them in a rented room for the first two years. When my sister attended the same high school, our parents rented an apartment.

I attended this school starting in ninth grade, right before my fifteenth birthday. My sister was in eleventh grade when I arrived, and my brother had graduated in the spring, but he was still living in Bacău, looking for a good job.

The cost of this schooling was not just a financial one to our family. It was also emotional, and Mom bore the brunt of it—although I wondered if I might have cried more than she did, at least in the beginning.

I will never forget my first day at the Bacău aeronautical technology high school. I was embarrassed to talk or even think about the episode at that time, but now looking back, I am not at all surprised at what happened.

I awoke homesick and nauseated with nerves. I sat on the edge of the bed staring out the third-floor apartment window. I was alone. Lenuța had already left for school, and Marin had gone out early with friends.

There were other tenants in the building, and possibly someone would have been available to console me, but embarrassment kept me from knocking on their doors. I could not call Mom and talk on the telephone, as we had no home phone, and though distraught, I was too proud to call the game and forest warden's wife and ask her to relay a message to my mother.

I was not too old to cry—so I cried.

I was mentally paralyzed in my room, captive to my own thoughts and fears, until my brother came back midmorning. After his pep talk and coaxing, I hesitantly walked to school, arriving late.

Mom came to visit by train every other week. Otherwise, when she was at home, she walked to the warden's home as often as she could to use their telephone to call us. Because my father and the warden were good friends, my mother and the warden's wife had developed amity as well. Both women had children the same age.

Mom's only other option for making calls was the public phone service offered in Iveşti, so she much preferred the privacy of the warden's home. She always lingered afterward to enjoy a cup of coffee with the warden's wife, feeding the flames of their friendship.

The archaic telephone system inside the National Telecom Company near the train station worked the same as the one in the warden's home, minus the cup of coffee. It required picking up the receiver and waiting for connection with an operator, who helped with both local and long-distance calling. The operator placed the call to the requested number, and the caller assumed the operator disconnected from the phone line once the two-party conversation was underway, but we always erred on the side of caution. We would never say anything of a personal nature that we didn't want a stranger to hear.

MARK LEE MYERS

Mom never came to Bacău empty-handed. She came bearing boxes of food—ingredients to fill our cupboards and pre-made meals to fill our bellies.

When she went home, we were responsible for cooking, washing clothes, getting up in the morning, and being disciplined to do our homework without the prodding of a parental figure in our rented apartment. However, we were still young, so being responsible did not mean the tasks always were completed. More adult supervision would have been best. I sometimes went to bed hungry, not because of any lack of food in the refrigerator and freezer or ingredients in the cupboard, but because of a lack of interest in cooking and cleaning.

———

Ours was not a normal adolescent life. One could focus on the differences and consider it a loss or a gain. But we did not lament what we did not have, what we could not do, or what needed to be done. Our parents set the tone for our outlook on life. They had much to complain about, but never did. How true their motto proved to be: "You will walk a straighter line if you focus on the goal."

We were not perfect children. I most certainly speak for myself and mean no disrespect to my brother and sister. We shared a love for our parents and a respect for our family heritage. The experience of attending high school in a distant city and working for a wage broadened our perspectives, but still, we knew there was no place like home.

29

Forgery

~ Fall 1986 ~

THE university entrance exam taken after graduating high school was designed to separate the wheat from the chaff, an analogy farmers like ourselves understood. If a male graduate passed the university test, he only had to serve six months in the military; otherwise, eighteen months. The exact military start date was not so important, as long as it was not put off for too long.

My brother failed on his first attempt. He couldn't retake the exam for one year, but he wanted to get a job before committing to his lengthier military service. He sought an interview at the Bacău military manufacturing plant, hoping his electronics education might land him an entry-level job. What he learned instead was another life lesson about the restrictions of communism.

A residency stamp was required for the county in which employment was sought, in order to get the proper work permit ID card. He could work a temporary position, such as an internship, without a residency stamp, but not anything full-time. To get a residency stamp, a person had to prove property ownership in the same county.

Some people were able to purchase extra property in situations like this because they had signed the communist allegiance papers, which allowed them to live under the radar. Our family was not on a favored list with the Communist authorities—quite the opposite—so it was near impossible to purchase more property.

Dad didn't take the word "no" kindly, especially from a Communist. He considered "no" to be a response, not an answer, so he began pursuing unconventional means of obtaining a residency stamp.

In our apartment building, we met a man who worked for the government. Not all government workers were corrupt by association, but in this particular case, the label of dishonesty would have applied.

This man heard our story and volunteered to help us bypass the residency stamp requirement and obtain our work permit ID cards for a healthy fee of twenty thousand *lei*. This was the nearly equivalent of twenty months' salary for the average citizen. We had to give him our passports, and he said it would take two weeks.

He kept his word on the timeframe, and he came back with the ID cards and returned our passports. The work permit ID cards were booklets similar to a passport with several pages.

My brother noticed the seal stamped in the work permit ID booklet looked odd. Dad took the work permit ID cards to a friend, who looked under a magnifying glass and confirmed the ID cards were not authentic. The residency stamp had been hand-drawn.

We felt devastated. A lot of money was lost, and the forged documents were illegal. We thought we had paid a bribe to elude the critical eye of those who had responsibility to confirm our proof of property ownership, but we did not think we were purchasing counterfeit work permit ID cards. We had expected the real deal.

The man we paid denied the forgery. The counterfeiters had preyed on innocent folks. Dad pressed the man hard to get our money back, but it was useless. He got scared and stopped talking to us. We knew we had lost the game and could not go to the police for help.

Dad did not surrender easily. He thought of an idea that did not have Mom's approval.

He burned the pocket portion of his jacket and burned half of each work permit ID card, the portion containing the forged stamp. He took the ID cards to the employment office in Bacău and showed them the "evidence" of the unfortunate loss. He asked for replacement residency ID cards—and replacements he got.

These were the real deal.

30

House Wine

~ Fall 1986 ~

A GLASS of wine can cure many ills. It is also a festive part of Romanian culture, in abundance at every celebration, and served with most meals.

Autumn was all about preservation: to protect the flavors of summer for enjoyment throughout the year and to prepare concoctions from crops using recipes perfected by patience. Fall weather brought a reprieve from the summer sun, with more rain, cooler days, and crisp nights. Time spent outside was invigorating, and more people lingered in the dusk, absorbing all they could of the day.

There were many things to preserve this time of year. The first frost, usually in mid-October, would stop the tomato growth overnight. We rushed to catch the ripened harvest before it plummeted and burst on the ground, and Mom started cooking and canning tomato sauces for the winter. We picked and pickled the green tomatoes we found still clinging to the stalk.

Mom's greatest pride of preserving was her artful distilment of grapes into wine. Dad had the green thumb of horticulture, and Mom had the purple thumb of vinification. Her house wine blend was smooth on the palate and soothing to the soul.

I appreciate even more now that my mother preserved the art and tradition of wine making, especially given that my grandparents had owned a beautiful winery and a several-acre vineyard, but by the time I was born, the government had confiscated the property for redistribution.

Dad planted our property with grape vines trellised on the fence line and arbors in the front yard. A pergola in the front yard hosted yellowish grapes best eaten plump off the vine. We harvested the trellised deep-red grapes in the fall. Our wine was fermented from these grapes.

The grapes grown on our farm were a rare variety not found for sale on the open market. The grape skins were sensitive and less conducive for transport. This was to our advantage, as it meant the skins would burst with flavor. These grapevine cultivars were handed down from generation to generation.

Mom made her "reserve" wine from the first press grape extract. Dad also bought grapes from other growers to augment production so we could produce a quantity of wine for ourselves and for friends, relatives, and neighbors.

Our region of Romania was famous for growing grapes. People who owned only a half-acre of land would commonly grow grapes, which was a crop the authorities did not try to regulate or restrict.

Dad circled through the countryside, with Simi trotting the way, wagon in tow, in search of the quality of grapes Mom insisted upon. Mom's famous flavor was a blend of white and red juice. Dad bought more than two metric tons of grapes, which he packaged in thirty-five-kilo thick plastic bags for ease of transport and handling.

Retaining field workers in the heat of summer was a challenge, but it seemed easier to solicit help with the winemaking in the fall. The weather and wine made for a festive spirit, and Dad allowed his hired help to imbibe on this particular job. No one was much interested in the fresh-pressed juice when the fermented vintage from last year was now aged to excellence.

Mom kept the home fires burning and the farm crew busy during tomato season when Dad and I made our travels to market, but the tomato season took me away from home repeatedly, so it was during the winemaking season that I saw more of Mom's intense focus.

We did not have the luxury of new wooden barrels for winemaking, so we repurposed existing barrels by cleaning them with boiling water mixed with dried cones of hops vines found twining in the wild. There was nothing easy about this cleaning method.

We sealed the large barrels, except for two holes, one at the bottom fitted with a spigot and one near the top fitted with a large cork. This allowed us to funnel the hops and hot water into the top hole, and then tip the barrel side-to-side, sloshing the water to rinse the interior.

Mom was fastidious about the barrel-cleaning process because of the ill effect unclean barrels could have on the taste of the final fermented product. Many conditions alter the delicacy of each vintage—soil nutrients absorbed into the vine roots, rainfall amounts, sunshine-to-shade ratios, and the timing of each during the separate stages of fruit growth and maturity. However, the barrel chemistry composition was as important to my mother as spices are to a master chef. Mom put her nose to the top hole after each barrel rinse until the smell was to her satisfaction.

The winemaking process commenced under the shade of a roof Dad built over the outdoor access to our underground cellar. We dumped grape clusters into a four-sided wooden funnel attached to the top of two long, grooved rollers. The funneled-bucket apparatus was mounted on two wooden two-by-four props and hoisted on top of a large, upside-down-cone-shaped wooden vat.

The top of this wooden vat was nearly eight feet in diameter and stood seven feet tall. A large cast iron wheel with a wooden handle rotated smaller gears behind it that turned the two aforementioned rollers in opposite directions, bursting the skins of the grapes and beginning the process of releasing the juice from the pulp.

Things looked bigger when I was small. The diameter of that cast iron crank wheel reminded me of a Ferris wheel. The first several hundred cranks were fun, but the last several hours were pure pain and boredom. Dad eventually hooked the crank wheel to an electric motor, but that was later in life—too late, in my opinion.

The liquid and pulp filled the wooden vat to within twelve to eighteen inches of the top, leaving room for expansion as the fermentation process swelled the contents. The air temperature and grape sugar content triggered the start of fermentation and controlled its intensity.

Abundant rainfall produces juicier grapes and more wine. But grapes are sweeter when the season is dryer and less so when summer rains are plentiful. The high sugar content in grapes grown where we lived caused an intense fermentation to begin immediately.

Mom repeatedly tested for quality of color and taste. The fresh grape juice, especially in this quantity, could turn sour quickly, ruining the whole batch. Mom dropped an egg into a pitcher of fresh-squeezed grape juice, and the egg floated if the sugar content was to her liking. If the egg did not float, she added sugar, but seldom was this necessary. Nothing artificial was added. Mom's recipe was nature's recipe.

Bubbles rumbled from the top of the pulp vat as the fermentation process worked its magic to release flavor and tannins. The aroma of grape skin tannins and fruit juice permeated the autumn air.

Mom believed that keeping the pulp and juice together as long as possible in the large vat was one secret to the best flavor. The longer the pulp was kept in this stage, the darker the wine. She looked for taste that did not pinch her tongue. In ideal weather conditions, when grape content was not overly sweet, the first fermentation in the large vat lasted two to three days.

After Mom separated and saved the first batch of her reserve wine, she added the purchased grapes to the process, and the fermentation restarted. When the bubbling subdued to an occasional burp, we gravity-drained the cloudy liquid, distributing it into seven wooden barrels, where it rested for several weeks out of direct sunlight.

Each of the seven wooden barrels was fitted with a cork that contained a center straw to channel the expanding gas into plastic bottles filled with water as the fermentation process slowed to completion. This prevented the air from mixing with the wine as the gas bubbles escaped.

When all sediment filtered to the bottom of the barrel, the wine became translucent. Mom siphoned the wine to a clean barrel, leaving the sediment for discard.

It required one final transfer to store the flavor of the season in the cellar for later consumption. To save our back muscles, we put the last empty barrels in the cellar and ran a long hose from the aboveground barrels to the empty ones below.

Many coveted Mom's wine. The hired help periodically requested payment for their services in bottles of wine. We also gave some bottles to the game warden, which ended up on the dining table at his home when the government elites visited from Bucharest during hunting season.

The government elites were part of an establishment that did little to lift the spirits of the Romanian people, but we used liquid spirits to merry the hearts of many. It was a twisted scenario in my mind—as if the communist motto was "give and from you shall be taken," but my parents were happy to make others happy.

My parents were givers, not takers.

31

Unwelcome Visit

~ Winter 1986 ~

THEY weren't invited, but that didn't stop them from coming.

The holiday festive season was a targeted time for the Communists to continue executing their plans for splintering the Cismigiu family morale and persecuting us for attempting to live a life free from its control. The authorities were unsuccessful in breaking the will of "Mr. Ionel Cismigiu" during the tomato planting and harvesting, so their focus this time of year was on his wife and children.

The police arrived unannounced in two patrol cars. There was power in numbers, so they never came alone.

The routine of their unwanted visit played out in similar fashion each time. Their premise was that the money made from the tomato harvest was illegal. In their rulebook, a landowner should not own so much land, and further, my parents were not permitted to use their land in the manner in which they did.

The heated conversation at the front doorstep started the same each visit. Dad answered the harsh knock and stepped outside, bursting their circle of comfort and closing the front door behind him. The officers took a step or two backward, not knowing how to interpret the boldness of the one they came to interrogate.

"Glad to see you," Dad lied. "I hope you are all here to help with the chores."

An officer snarled. "We have permission to search your house for illegal money."

"You will find no illegal money in this home, because I have not conducted any illegal business. I don't respect your accusation. Who is the coward that granted you permission to enter without my invite?" Dad's tone was fearless and firm.

A hand thrust forward, presenting papers drawn up by a Communist-loyal judge who gave them the "right" of entry.

Dad had no choice but to allow them entry. Even though I had a knot in my stomach, I was also amused watching each officer step across the threshold. Dad stood to one side, just outside the door, which required each man to pass within arm's reach of him and step inside with their back exposed. More than one darted a sideward glance, looking nervous and intimidated.

They ransacked most everything, taking contents out of the drawers and closets and from under the beds. They lifted the mattresses, emptied the refrigerator, looked inside the stove, and made a total mess while searching for a money stash. But my father was much smarter than they ever gave him credit. He knew better than to keep his money where they could find it. And he knew better than to keep it in our home. The police probably knew they would not find what they searched for, but they were relentless in their theatrical pursuit.

If Dad would not and could not be broken to submit, they hoped to splinter the morale of his wife and children. Household contents were ransacked, and bed sheets, towels, and clothing were often taken outside and thrown in the dirty snow.

Arrogance swelled proportionate to the length of their stay as they executed their intentions slowly and methodically. By the time they ended their tirade, their body language as they swaggered to their cars strongly indicated that they had accomplished their *real* mission once again. We had no doubt they would be back.

After they left, Dad vented his frustration by stomping back and forth on the hardwood floor and ranting about "Commies." Dad was strong-willed and more hardened and determined by each encounter.

Mom had the sensitivity one would expect from the caretaker of the family home. She was humiliated and embarrassed but never let the intruders have the satisfaction of seeing her cry. But when she went to clean up the mess, tears rolled down her cheeks. It took days to return things to normal, but in time, we made the house feel like home again.

32

Ice Cream Overdose

~ Summer 1987 ~

KIDS love ice cream, and I was no different. But too much of a good thing can still be too much.

The summer after Dad's health scare, he and I were well into our routine by midseason. It was time to rotate our travels to another market city.

The city of Reghin, in the north-center of Romania, covers both sides of the Mureş River and bustles with commerce, which is the reason Dad originally selected this alternate destination to market his tomatoes. The city had not one, but three, farmer's markets.

As we drove the roads or rode the rails flowing into this city, we understood why. Reghin lies near the edge of a fertile high-elevation plateau. To the east, fifteen miles away, the Carpathian Mountains provide the backdrop; to the west, farmland patches the rolling countryside for at least sixty-five miles toward the city of Cluj-Napoca.

Romanian artisanship is on grand display in Reghin. The architecture, reminiscent of Transylvanian tradition, is ornate, intricate, and gilded, often trimmed with wrought-iron balconies and crowned with steeple spires on rooflines. Craftsmen still practice medieval trades, and the city is well known for making musical instruments, especially violins. The nearby Călimani Forest supplies a resonant wood that is used to make these musical instruments world famous. The quaint city radiates a delightful ambiance—a pleasant fragrance of the past.

We'd discovered this market mecca a few years earlier, and this season, Dad saw an opportunity for sales growth. His idea was to double sales in half the time: I would manage a booth at the train station while he managed the traditional setup at one of the three city markets.

Hundreds, if not thousands, of people buzzed around the train station, especially during peak periods when people traveled home from work. Dad surmised it might be a good idea to offer travelers an easier option to buy tomatoes as they crisscrossed the train station, eliminating the extra walk to and from the city market.

There was no formal farmer's market inside the train station or along the platform. There were a few empty tables long abandoned and sitting idle, so Dad came up with a plan.

When we arrived in the early morning, we hired a man with a horse and wagon to transfer our cargo to the farmer's market at the city center where we unloaded all but fifteen tomato crates. Dad rented one booth and two scales: one for each of us. We setup Dad's booth for business, and the hired help took me back to the train station where I setup my sales operation with the remaining product.

I set the scale on top of the abandoned train station table and stacked the tomato crates on the floor. No one questioned if I had permission to use the table or had spoken to any authorities for approval to sell at this location. We operated under the premise that asking for permission first might be more difficult than asking for forgiveness later.

The idea caught on quickly. The line swelled to over seventy-five people in a matter of minutes without a single word of advertisement. Half of the customers were Hungarian, so in no time, I learned to speak enough of the language for selling.

I sold out early and walked back to the city-center market, leaving my empty crates but carrying the scale and cast-iron weights. I was not concerned about anyone stealing the empty crates, but the scale was a rented item that could easily come up missing if left unattended. The two-mile distance didn't seem far when I started out, but I forgot to take into consideration the cumbersome apparatus.

I stayed to help Dad for the remainder of the afternoon in the city market. Sales were not brisk—too much competition. He wished now that he had given me more crates. It was too late in the afternoon to return to the train station to bolster our sales. This would be a two-day venture.

After the market closed, Dad paid the horse-and-wagon driver to go back to the train station and get the empty crates I had left. We closed our booth and tied our crates together.

It was common for out-of-town farmers to sleep overnight in the market. Many a night, our booth was our bed, but even when it was not, there were enough people around the market at night that we trusted our product would not be stolen. We never had a problem.

A friend of my father owned a home at the edge of the city. I don't know how he met the man, but no one was ever a stranger for long with my father, so I'm sure it was probably a handshake, a bit of storytelling, and mutual admiration.

The man had many family members living in his home, and a married son living in a small structure erected in the courtyard, so there were no extra bedrooms. He invited us to sleep in the barn, but with use of the bathroom facilities. We arrived late, lifted the gate latch, and entered the barn. We paid him in tomatoes the next morning.

A creek ran next to his property, and the musical trickling of water over stones should have lulled us to sleep. But the creek was likely the source of *huge* mosquitoes. We had no bug spray to provide a protective layer of repellent. If someone had been watching, it would have looked like Dad and I practiced karate moves as we swatted and sliced the air attempting to thwart the aerial strikes from the swarms of mosquitoes.

We finally covered our heads with a blanket. The mosquito activity died down sometime during the night, but by then, the bloodsucking needles with wings had won the battle, and red dots speckled our cheeks the next morning.

There are memories engraved in my mind of summers spent in Reghin, but the one that saddens me most is one that should've made me most happy—and it would have if I had not overdosed.

The morning after our inaugural test marketing at the train station, Dad again split up our two-man team, sending me back to peddle tomatoes to the train travelers while he opened up his booth at city-central market.

My danger was not from external sources. The danger was from within. Indulgence.

There was an ice cream stand at the train station, and I was a kid unsupervised. I had tasted ice cream before, but only on limited occasions and in limited supply.

I had money in my pocket and what seemed like an endless supply of ice cream to purchase. The ice cream was replenished from a delivery truck each morning. Like my tomato marketing plan, the ice cream vendor's business was done for the day when the product was sold out. This put a sense of urgency on me to eat fast and buy often.

I have never found a better waffle cone than the ones freshly baked at this treat shop. They were a little softer and a lot more flavorful. Dad had given me a sandwich to take with me, so I didn't need to fend for food. But one scoop of ice cream led to another, and soon I lost track of the number of times I frequented the counter.

Unlike a bartender with a sense of responsibility to help a customer know when to stop consumption by refusing service, the ice cream salesclerk fed my addiction. I ate so much that I got sick, but I never shared the reason why with my father.

Too much of anything, even something good, can be a bad thing. To this day, I don't like vanilla ice cream.

33

Faster Pace

~ Summer 1987 ~

I AWOKE with the sun filling my bedroom window, which surprised me since one of my parents usually woke me before sunrise on workdays. The extra two days on the last mountain train ride had weakened my stamina. Of course, my parents didn't know that my sickly countenance was partly due to my ice cream overdose.

The house was quiet, but I heard voices near the barn. I rubbed my eyes and yawned. Had Dad left without me?

I had seen the mountain of filled tomato crates stacked in the barn when unhitching Simi from the wagon the night before. Dad and I had had to walk the two and a half miles home from the train station, leaving the empty crates stacked against the side of the building, and had taken the horse and wagon back to get them, returning well after dark to unload them in the corner of the barn.

There were more filled crates than usual in the barn, but in the darkness, I had been too tired to count them. Maybe I had been a bit delirious from the long travels and ice cream-induced stomachache. Maybe it had been my imagination. Maybe it had been a dream. It felt more like a nightmare. The tomato harvest season was dragging on, and I was tired of traveling.

I swung my feet out of bed and sat up on the edge. My mental fog was dissolving in the sunrays streaming through the window, and I started to think a little clearer. A mountain of filled tomato crates meant we could not postpone a trip to the mountain market. The train left at ten a.m., and it felt like it might be close to that time now. Maybe Marin had gone with Dad today.

I walked to the kitchen, hoping to find breakfast leftovers to satisfy the tiger in my tummy. Out the kitchen window, I could see Marin and a hired hand carrying crates from the barn to the main gate. They were not working with the usual urgency.

"Good morning, sunshine!" Mom opened the porch screen door and entered with a pail half-filled with fresh chicken eggs. "I wondered how long you might sleep."

"Good morning, Mom. Has Dad already left for the train station?"

"No. The two of you are not going by train today. Your dad hired a man with a truck and trailer to take you there much faster. There might be more police checkpoints, but fewer train stations to stop at along the way."

I forced a frown and shrugged. I was game for a new adventure. "What time do we leave?" I asked.

"The driver will be here with the trailer at about six-thirty p.m. Hurry and eat breakfast so you can help haul the tomato crates to the main gate. There are a lot of chores to catch up on today." I heard what she said, but I moved slowly, hoping my brother and the hired help would finish the task before I got outside.

The remnants of breakfast I found were typical of our usual summer morning meals: sausage preserved from the winter pig slaughter; bread; hard-boiled eggs; feta cheese, which Mom made fresh or bought from local shepherds; and fresh tomatoes salted and arranged on a plate in the middle of the table.

I loved the sights and sounds flowing in through the open windows. It was rare to sit inside alone on a workday morning and relax.

Fulga darted past the windowpane playfully chasing the barn cat. The other farm dog, Rex, was already in the shade of a tree watching the chase with his chin resting on his paw, and there was no indication he was the least bit interested in joining the romp.

These two dogs were vastly different. Fulga loved work and play. It was bred into him. The night Fulga bounded into my life came flashing back. I laughed at myself, remembering how the "White Ghost" had frightened me at first.

Our farm always bustled with animals. Once Dad caught a wild boar piglet in the woods and brought it home. We kept it for a week. It got loose and ran back to the woods, but not before it tangled several times with our dogs. It had a very different personality from the domestic pig we fattened each year for the holiday slaughter. The wild pig's instinct was to defend itself and its territory. It was no wonder both Simi and I were frightened on my first midnight ride to market with Dad through the darkened forest when the wild boar spooked us.

Another time, Dad rescued a wounded pheasant and brought it home, where we hand-fed it for a week before it died. A taxidermist friend of the family preserved it, and the lifelike pheasant still hung on the living room wall.

Marin walked from the barn with the last tomato crate, and the hired hand started on another job. It was probably time I headed outside.

I could not see Dad and assumed he was directing chores from a location somewhere in the barn. If I did not show up soon, Dad might dispatch someone to find me. It would be better if I appeared of my own free will. I had already been gifted the extra sleep this morning. I should not push my luck.

I entered the barn, and Dad glanced over his shoulder, raised his eyebrows, and teased, "I wondered if you might sleep all day."

I continued walking toward him and feigned a smile. "It was a nice surprise. Thanks. I needed it."

I glanced over my shoulder at the stack of tomato crates repositioned by our front gate. It had not been my imagination. Another eighty-three tomato crates were ready for market, the result of harvest two days prior.

Warm, gentle rains had blanketed the Siret River Valley two weeks earlier, falling at a steady rate, which allowed deep penetration into the dry tomato field rather than wasted runoff to the Bârlad River. The water had reached the thirsty plants' roots, which absorbed the liquid like a sponge.

Four hundred kilos of tomatoes filled ten extra tomato crates. Another picking would be ripe in a day or two, and it promised an above-average abundance as well.

Mom could only cook, stew, and preserve so many. Even the chickens and ducks that meandered freely around our farm were getting tired of tomatoes. At the start of the harvest season, both two-footed specimens fought for first place at the compost pile where imperfect tomatoes that Mom could not use were discarded. They were not bothered by the rotting aroma, but pecked and plucked until their white heads were stained tomato-red. But by this time of the bountiful harvest, these animals avoided the taste of tomatoes like the plague.

I was about to ask, but Dad spoke first.

"We are going back to the mountains today ... a different way. I walked into town last night after you went to bed and talked to a man I know who is willing to take us up there using his vehicle and trailer.

"The tomatoes are ripening fast, and they will pick another full load in a few days. The recent rains are producing more tomatoes—and larger ones.

"I think this option might get us there faster. We won't have to stop at every train station or handle the crates twice at the Ciceu station."

It seemed to make sense. Dad was not asking for my verbal approval, so I nodded.

"Mom said we leave this evening. Why not start earlier?"

"I talked to Costache, the man I hired to take us. I think you will recognize him. We agreed it might be safer at night."

"Safer?" I frowned and furrowed my brow.

"Yes. We'll blend in better with other traffic on the road. We'll be driving on roads that basically go the same route as the train, but the checkpoints are different ..." He raised an eyebrow. "... with different inspectors. I'm hoping even the inspectors will be sleepier at night."

I snorted in amusement.

Dad smiled. "I hope the inspectors like tomatoes. I'll try offering them some. Hopefully they won't demand too much money. We'll see how it goes."

I enjoyed the small talk. It was saving me from having a chore assigned, but the reprieve soon ended.

"I think your mother already gathered the eggs this morning. Grab a pitchfork and start cleaning out Simi's stall. Make sure the dogs and cats have food. It is hot, so be sure their water is in the shade. When you're done, join the others in the field and ask your mother for a task."

I worked at a steady pace, but I didn't try to set any record. The day dragged by, but I liked it slower.

The driver my father had hired pulled up at the main gate a few minutes after six-thirty and honked his horn. The horn was not necessary. I had heard his empty trailer rattling over road ruts long before he arrived.

He was not driving a truck as I expected. His vehicle was an ARO 243, a Romanian-built utility vehicle, a bit smaller than a truck, patterned after the boxy English Land Rover. Instead of an open cargo truck bed, it had an enclosed cargo area behind the passenger seat. The roof over the cargo space had a higher profile than that over the driver and front passenger seating area. It was built to endure rugged off-road terrain but, to me, it looked too small to pull the trailer.

"Hello, Costache."

"Hello, Cuţa."

I did not remember seeing the man before, but I assumed Dad must have known him enough to trust him to help us. The man addressed my father by the nickname "Cuţa." His friends usually did.

"Do you think it is going to rain on us?" Costache asked. "I don't have a tarp."

Dad smiled. "Rain won't hurt the tomatoes. It will wash them again and make them prettier to sell."

Obviously, this man was not a farmer, or maybe he was making casual small talk. It did cause me to look toward the mountains. It was clear and sunny where we stood, but clouds were heavy with rain far to the north.

"I think the rain will be gone by nightfall," Dad said confidently. "The road might be wet, that's all."

This was a reasonable forecast. The prevailing winds surged over the Transylvanian Plateau collecting moisture, and then were trapped swirling inside the western slopes of the fishhook-shaped Carpathian Mountain range. By the time the air mass was ridge-lifted to the upper atmosphere, moisture was usually wrung out, saturating the landmass below. The clouds that toppled over the mountain peaks and spilled into the Siret River Valley usually contained less water, and the resulting rain showers were short-lived. But Dad's forecast didn't ease a concern swelling in the pit of my stomach. Something felt ominous about this trip. I glanced again at the looming clouds.

Dad, Marin, two gypsies, Costache, and I diminished the stack of tomato crates like ants on a sugar mound. A steady stream of crates flowed into the trailer from all sides, filling it to capacity in minutes. There were still full tomato crates remaining by the gate.

Dad bit his lower lip while glancing at the trailer and the remaining stack. "That makes seventy-two crates on the trailer, and the wheels don't look like they will allow any more, even if there were room on top."

No one spoke, and no one offered an alternative, but it seemed obvious that Dad was pondering an idea. He walked over to the vehicle, opened the rear door, and squatted, squinting at something under the two long bench seats facing each other.

"We can remove these two back seats," he suggested, more to himself than anyone else.

He reached in to feel for how the seats were fastened. "There are four bolts," he confirmed, and then pointed toward the barn.

"Marin, run and get a wrench from the toolbox. Bring them all. I think there are three sizes." He had not waited for Costache to approve or protest the seat removal. It was a logical solution to him. "Also bring a rope to tie down the crates in the trailer," he shouted toward Marin, who had already sprinted halfway to the barn.

Costache sauntered toward the open vehicle door. His lips parted, but no sound came out.

"I'll put it back together good as new when we return," Dad said.

Marin ran back with two wrenches in hand and a long rope slung over his shoulder. "I could find only these two." He handed the larger one to Dad.

In less than ten minutes, the back seats sat on the ground beside the ARO. At Dad's instructions, Marin and I carried the seats toward the barn, one gypsy brought the unpacked tomato crates to the ARO, and the other gypsy and Costache secured the previously loaded crates to the trailer using the rope.

"I wonder where Dad expects me to sit if he fills the back seat area with crates," I commented to Marin as we walked toward the barn. I glanced back over my shoulder.

Dad was already a thought ahead. He had filled the ARO cargo trunk with tomato crates, every inch of available space packed tightly from floor to ceiling. He had placed one crate in the middle on the floorboard for me to sit on, leaving a gap between the front two seats and the middle console for my feet, and then stacked crates on either side up tight against each side door.

When I leaned inside and saw where I'd be sitting, I darted back into the house to fetch a blanket to give me a little padding. *Was this safe? What if we had a wreck? Would I be crushed under a pile of tomato crates or drowned in a sea of tomato juice?*

No sense worrying, I consoled myself. I climbed in through the front seat and contorted my body into the cubbyhole. With Dad in the passenger seat and Costache at the wheel, the motorized tomato wagon pulled away from the main gate. Costache was tall and thin, Dad was short and stocky. And so the portrait of the two men framed through the windshield must have appeared lopsided. Mom, Lenuța, Marin, and the two gypsies waved goodbye. Cuța and Costache waved back. I waved … but knew no one could see me.

I had heard of the phrase "tunnel vision," and I was experiencing it now firsthand. Slits between the tomato crates allowed a little light to shine through, but unless I leaned forward, I could only see straight out the front window. It would be dark soon, and there would not be much to see anyway. Even though sleep was hours away, I wished I had grabbed another blanket to use as a pillow. I might have to sacrifice seating comfort for a headrest when that time came.

34

Checkpoint Savvy

~ Summer 1987 ~

NAVIGATING through the police checkpoints required bribes and bravery. The first checkpoint, often the worst one, was located right at the county line immediately on our side of the river outside the town of Cosmeşti.

To get there, we drove north to the city of Tecuci, passing through several smaller towns en route. I had traveled through these towns many times on the train with my father, and I was now enjoying seeing what I could of them from my narrow view through the front window of the vehicle. The road had paralleled the train tracks on the right ever since we left Torceşti, but as we entered Tecuci, the train tracks angled to the west, and we crossed over them to enter town.

Tecuci covered almost twice the landmass as Focşani, the mountain city where we sold our tomatoes at the start of the season, but it had one-third the population. That was another reason why Focşani had been a better choice for marketing our tomatoes.

The residents of Tecuci had attempted to spruce up their city by planting trees in what was originally flat grazing grass, so some streets of Tecuci were lined with trees, trimmed to form an arch over the roadway. Similar to my hometown, the houses were built close to the street, and most had a fence around the yard ornately designed to be different from the neighbors'. The fences in Torceşti were mostly wooden; here in Tecuci, many were constructed of stone, brick, and iron.

As we left Tecuci, the highway angled northwest toward Cosmeşti, and we met back up with the train tracks, which now were on the left side of the road. This should have been familiar terrain as we'd passed this way so often on train travels, but it occurred to me that at this point in the train ride, Dad and I were busy inside the parcel boxcar sorting out the mess caused by our hasty loading back at the Iveşti station. It was normally not until we got to the river crossing that we had restacked our tomato crates with some semblance of order and we could take note of the passing scenery. This was flat land, good for grazing, and the setting sun highlighted a shepherd with his flock as specks of white off in the distance.

The river was now straight ahead. I reminisced about my first approach to the Siret River in the blackness of night with my father and a horse-drawn wagon full of crated tomatoes. Apprehension had been as thick as darkness, and strangely, I felt a similar feeling now. But why?

I glanced at Dad, who seemed deep in thought. I wanted to ask him a question but realized he was focused straight ahead. I followed his line of sight and saw why he was attentive. We were about to be tested at the first police checkpoint. A large metal bridge, double-stacked with two platforms, spanned the river. Only trains traversed the river on the upper deck tracks, and everything else crossed by way of the bottom deck roadway: pedestrians, motorized vehicles, bicycles, and horse-drawn carts.

This checkpoint was set up right before the entrance to the lower deck of the bridge. The train tracks on the upper deck were level with the surrounding riverbank, so access to the lower-deck roadway was via a ramp off to the right that curved down and around the bridge pylon. This slowed the traffic approaching the bridge, allowing the police to survey and predetermine whom to stop and interrogate.

Our motorized tomato wagon stood out as a target. No question we would be chosen for inspection. If permission to proceed was not granted, there was little chance of us getting across the river, and we risked being arrested or fined. The closest bridge to the north accessible by major road was sixty miles away, and doubtless it had a police roadblock. To the south, there was a small, old, and possibly unsafe bridge near Lungoci, some thirty miles or more. There was, of course, the clandestine barge crossing somewhere in the middle of nowhere, only accessible by horse.

"What do you have for them?" Costache questioned my father.

"We have lots of tomatoes. I'll start with that. We'll see how hungry they are."

It was a serious statement, but the two men smiled at the irony. There sure were many tomatoes on board.

"You could say they are coming out our ears," I blurted out.

The three of us burst out laughing. It was funny to see the tomato crates enveloping my head. The outburst released the tension, which had built up in our cramped space.

We were behind a row of other vehicles that inched toward the inspector on duty. The driver's side window was rolled down because the vehicle had no air-conditioning. Costache kept both hands on the steering wheel and pulled to a stop when the police officer raised his hand.

"What have we here?" the policeman began. "And where are you heading?"

Costache did not speak. He was waiting for Dad to explain. Dad leaned over the middle console so that the officer could make eye contact with him.

"Good evening, officer," Dad said. "We are heading to the mountains with a load of tomatoes."

The officer quite possibly had never seen a setup like this before. He bent down and peered inside. He grinned a crooked smile when he saw me sandwiched between tomato crates, and then shook his head. It was difficult to tell if he might let us go or if he was stalling for a bribe. Dad reached for a bag of tomatoes he had tucked by his feet, handed it to Costache, who in turn extended it out his window.

"Officer, these are the best vine-ripe tomatoes you have ever tasted. Compliments from me to you," Dad said.

The officer locked his grip around the top of the bag, and Costache released his hold on the bottom. The officer slowly bobbed the bag up and down, puckered his lips, and furrowed his brow. He was either impressed with the weight of the tomatoes or contemplating if this one bagful was a sufficient bribe.

Dad did not wait to find out. He reached down and produced the second of two bags he had prepared. He had hoped to save this one for another checkpoint, but he offered it now without hesitation. Costache took it from Dad and extended it out his window like the first.

The officer grabbed it with his spare hand, then stood there looking like a kid who might have gotten both hands caught in the cookie jar. Maybe he was hungry or maybe he felt compassion for us, but for some reason, this police officer accepted the two bags of tomatoes and waved us on.

We pulled onto the lower deck of the bridge, and I leaned forward, straining to see out the side windows. The river fascinated me. I no longer was spooked by it like the first time many years earlier when I crossed it on a barge in the dead of night somewhere far to the south.

We entered Vrancea County, and a quick five miles later, we navigated the second police checkpoint at Tişiţa.

Tişiţa is a small spot on a map where three roadways meet. The busy crossroads were a prime location for the police to monitor travel and transport. This was not a border crossing into a foreign country, where national sovereignty was paramount to protect. This was the heartland of Romania. I did not understand much at this young age about politics or governmental affairs, but the innocence of youth speaks the truth so simply.

"Dad, what are the police afraid of?"

Dad did not immediately answer. He was staring out the front window. His furrowed brow told me he might be pondering how the incident looming ahead at the next police checkpoint might play out.

MARK LEE MYERS

I continued before I got an answer, "We lock our doors at home to keep people outside from coming in. It seems like the police want to keep us locked in … so we can't get out."

The purity of that thought resonated like a strike of a tuning fork: a perfect tone. Neither my father nor Costache responded.

The police traffic control tower was on an island in the center of the intersection. This circle of mounded earth, around which all the intersecting roads convened, allowed for a continual flow of merging traffic. Continual, that is, unless the police motioned for a vehicle to pull over into one of the curbside parking areas prior to the intersection.

From the control tower vantage point, approaching traffic could be examined by the naked eye or with the aid of binoculars. Vehicles heavily laden like our ARO 243 were easily recognizable from a good distance. By the time our motorized tomato wagon arrived, intending to turn north onto Highway E85, a police inspector was standing at ground level motioning for us to pull over and park.

The police officer swaggered toward our vehicle with a stone-faced expression. I wondered if Dad and Costache had knots in their stomachs like I did. There was no casual conversation through the open vehicle window or smirks of surprise from having seen the mass of tomato crates inside, as there had been at the prior checkpoint. The police officer ordered us to turn the vehicle engine off and step out.

He demanded documents faster than we could produce them: driver's license, vehicle registration, proof of road tax payment, and declaration of travel permits. Costache presented the first two without hesitation, struggled to find the third, and was empty-handed on the fourth. Neither he nor my father had filed for approval to transport the tomato harvest outside Galați County, because approval would have been rejected outright.

"You have no authority to be here," sneered the police officer, crossing his arms.

He did not ask for an explanation of how we had crossed the bridge five miles earlier. He knew. He was well aware how the system worked, and he was anxious to find out how much these submissive travelers would be willing to bribe him for another rite of passage.

This was going to be more difficult than Dad had planned, but traveling by train had become increasingly difficult as well. While Dad had established a good network of acquaintances along the train transport route, most of whom had long ago established a willing price for their service, the system was trying harder to crack down on his success; many of his accomplices faced increased pressure to prevent him from beating the system.

This particular police officer had never seen or heard of "Mr. Cismigiu" before. At least *that* was in Dad's favor, but it was apparent that the officer saw a ripe opportunity to collect a good settlement.

"Your Honor," Dad said, elongating each word and raising his eyebrows. "We are simply trying to take a very good commodity to very good people, fellow citizens." He hoped to appeal to any trace of decency in this officer's heart.

"Let me confer with my superiors and cross-reference some paperwork. You stay right here and do not get back in your vehicle." The officer turned, walked slowly back across the roadway to the control tower, and climbed the steps.

We knew he had no superiors to talk with or papers to cross-reference. This was a delay tactic used to make a person fear that the situation was escalating to a higher and more serious level, one that undoubtedly could be controlled by offering a larger bribe.

Costache paced nervously. He was not accustomed to this level of interrogation, as he was normally not driving contraband goods to market. Dad did not pace at all. He stood, shoulders erect, arms folded, glaring toward the control tower. My nerves had been growing weaker, but Dad's confidence encouraged me to feel stronger.

The officer waited a long time before returning, probably taking time to smoke a cigarette or two while watching the reactions of his quarry standing on the roadside and trying to assess their resolve.

MARK LEE MYERS

When he did return, he addressed "Mr. Cismigiu," whom he had correctly determined was the mastermind of this mission even from the passenger seat of the ARO 243.

"I do not yet have authority to let you proceed," he started. "I have made inquiry, and I believe there will be trouble."

On the outer northwest side of the circle intersection stood a Victory Monument of the first female Romanian lieutenant, Ecaterina Teodoroiu, who had bravely fought and died in World War I. She had been a nurse near the battlefront, but when she learned of her brother's death on the battlefield, she decided she must pick up his standard and serve her beloved country in her brother's honor. The bronze sculpture immortalized her standing with sword held high above her head, ready for battle.

"The bronze statue, over there," Dad pointed with straight arm and a stiff finger. "Have you forgotten what it symbolizes?" Dad glared directly into the officer's eyes. "She represents heroism. She saw the patriotism of those fallen soldiers on the front lines of the battlefield and asked herself the question 'What can I do to help?'" He paused for effect without blinking and continued, "Tonight, you have the same opportunity."

I had never heard this story before. I was impressed with the history lesson and with my father's clever appeal to Romanian national pride.

The officer was speechless. He had not been trained to defend a position from this angle. He had expected to extract a large monetary "tax" considering the number of tomato crates he had observed weighing down both the trailer and vehicle.

Dad sensed a softening in the officer's shell of armor and decided to close the deal before the armor hardened again. He walked to the rear of the ARO 243, opened the cargo door, and set out two full crates of tomatoes. He picked up one crate and motioned for Costache to get the other, then walked straight across the roadway with Costache in tow, leaving the officer standing on the roadside speechless. They stacked the tomato crates at the foot of the control tower stairs, and the two men walked back.

A bribe normally was transacted in a more clandestine manner. Often the trunk of a nearby police car was left open as an unspoken reminder of where to make payment.

"You can share those as you wish," Dad said. "We hope to see you again on a return trip." He didn't offer a handshake, but he did add, "And maybe we can bring a few other treats of interest for you next time. We will come more prepared."

This was a direct insinuation that a better gift might be afforded and available the next time they met, but it stopped short of labeling the current or future offering as a "bribe."

With Dad taking the lead, we climbed back into our vehicle without asking permission and pulled away from the roadside, turning north onto Highway E85. We drove in silence for a few miles, and then Costache glanced sideways at my father and spoke.

"Cuṭa, I am so impressed with what you did. I was worried—very worried. My mind froze with fear as he was up in the control tower glaring down at us. I felt helpless. But when he came back ... it all seemed to happen so fast. You took charge and changed the picture.

"I think he might still be standing back there wondering what just happened. I do know that for the first time in a very long time, I felt my dignity restored. That took courage. Thank you."

Dad politely shook his head. "Communism keeps people living in a box, which the government and police control. One must sometimes find a way outside the box."

35

Wreck On the Road

~ Summer 1987 ~

THE view on this side of the river was much like the other for the first ten miles, except that the road now paralleled the Siret River and a stand of trees and low shrubs hugged the riverbank, hiding it from view. We passed safely through several small villages, where most residents had retreated indoors for the evening.

The city of Adjud was well traveled by road and rail. A major train station was located there, which Dad and I passed through on every rail excursion. It was a major junction point with a labyrinth of switching tracks juggling the large volume of commercial and passenger rail traffic flowing through it.

The roadway also forked in the downtown square. Travel could either head west to ascend the steep ravines and slice through to the interior of the eastern Carpathian Mountains or continue north on a more gradual ascent to skirt the mountains en route to major destinations at Bacău, Roman, and eventually Suceava.

On prior trips, our train transport sometimes took the left fork to access the mountain towns as quickly and directly as possible, but the ARO 243 continued on the northerly road this evening. Dad had chosen the same market destination, Vatra Dornei, that we often had frequented by rail. He did not want to gamble traveling to a new location on this trip, and he was unsure how the motorized tomato wagon would fare on the long journey this night. He felt more comfortable taking the circuitous, more gradual ascent to skirt the mountains for as long as possible.

It was a good idea we chose this gradual-incline route into the Carpathian Mountains. The ARO 243 had a diesel engine that sounded much tougher than it really was. It struggled to handle the weight of the trailer filled to capacity. The interior compartment, crammed with additional crates and three comrades, added danger to the driving. On uphill climbs, the ARO 243 strained to maintain a minimum speed, often causing a long line of traffic to back up behind it, but it wasn't the slowest vehicle on the road.

Highway E85 was a major thoroughfare starting at the Ukraine border, north of the city of Siret and continuing south nearly three hundred miles to the city of Buzău. A variety of motorized vehicles, bicycles, and horse-drawn carts shared it. At times Costache had to try to pass even slower-moving vehicles. The risk was not only the varying speed, but his trailer did not have a sway bar, so any gust of air from a passing vehicle or a mountain pass, or any sudden movement when changing lanes, rocked the vehicle and trailer almost out of control.

Pull-offs scattered along the route were only large enough to accommodate a few vehicles, so Dad's plan was to drive most of the night with a stop around midnight at a famous restaurant, called Hanul Ancuței. Most people traveling this road day or night stopped there because it was open twenty-four hours. It was a good place, about the only place, to buy something to eat and relax, and fortunately for us, it had a huge parking lot.

The road north darkened faster as the mountains, towering to the west, cast long shadows on the foothills and farmland to the east. I was getting tired sooner than I had expected. The rocking of the road and the swaying of the vehicle lulled me to surrender to heavy eyelids.

––––––––

We made good time traveling and arrived at Hanul Ancuței about half past midnight. Costache found an accommodating parking space while Dad went inside to buy food and drinks, Costache inspected his trailer. I was glad to be out of my cage. My butt felt numb and my head sore from bouncing off wooden slats.

MARK LEE MYERS

"Looks like everything is riding well," Costache confirmed when Dad returned with the refreshments.

"Great. Let's get some food in our stomachs, and then take a short nap," Dad suggested. "I want to arrive at the Vatra Dornei market when the sun comes up. We don't have much farther to travel, but it might be more strenuous from this point as we head deeper into the mountains."

We ate sitting in the open air, then got back into the ARO 243. Costache and Dad laid their heads on the doorframe and tried to sleep. We were at a higher elevation, and the night air felt cool. I leaned against the crates and used my seat blanket for a little warmth.

The journey to and from market had become routine and somewhat monotonous to me. The weight of responsibility rested mainly on Dad's shoulders, allowing me to fall asleep ensconced in my recessed tomato-crate recliner in the center of the ARO.

————

The nap was shorter than I had hoped, and not that restful anyway. We pulled out of the rest area and continued our journey around two a.m. An hour or so later, we turned off to the left before Fălticeni onto roadway 2E, which would merge with A17 before Gura Humorului.

The road from Gura Humorului to Vatra Dornei was the most treacherous, and we would be traveling this last stretch of road right before daybreak, but we had to get to Gura Humorului first. That was many miles away, and I was already considering this mode of transportation more difficult, at least from my vantage point cramped in my tomato-crate crypt. This trip did not feel right for many reasons. My eyelids lost the battle to stay open, and I surrendered once again.

————

"What is the idiot trying to do?" Costache shouted, startling me awake. "He's going to cause a wreck!"

Costache's eyes darted from his side mirror to the logging truck ahead of us on the winding road. Dad leaned to catch a glimpse in the passenger-side mirror. I peered through the crevices between the tomato crates.

Costache shouted, "He keeps trying to pass us both at the same time."

"There's not enough time to get around both of us," Dad said.

Costache sounded worried. "He's driving like a maniac!"

As we approached Gura Humorului, it was evident that rain had swept through earlier in the night, leaving a sheen on the pavement. The two-lane road was curvy and sloped uphill. The early-morning rush was beginning as people scurried to work, and to make traffic worse, there were many logging trucks full of timber congesting the road.

We entered the east side of the city and slowly crawled along with the traffic. Costache could no longer see the car following from his side mirror, as the driver was riding too close to our trailer.

As we started to exit the far side of city, the driver in the vehicle behind us saw an opportunity to pass. He stomped on the gas pedal and darted out from behind.

The blast sounded like a gunshot, and I flinched, turning sideways in my seat. Through the slits between crates out the rear window, I saw the other vehicle hurtling through the air toward our trailer.

We would find out later that as the car behind us accelerated to pass, a dog had stepped from the side of the road, and the driver swerved to miss hitting it. The driver's reaction was over-corrective, and his car struck the curb and blew a tire. The car ricocheted like a torpedo and struck our trailer with a thud.

The impact blew our left trailer tire. The trailer flipped upside down, torqueing our vehicle on its side. The ARO scraped across the pavement while tilted on the driver's side and front-left hood panel. The driver's door smashed on impact, but the tomato crates helped keep the roof from collapsing.

It happened fast but seemed like slow motion. I braced myself against tomato crates as our vehicle went through acrobatics. Sparks shot up from under the wedged metal. The ARO uncoiled and flipped upright. Our vehicle and upside-down tomato trailer came to rest diagonally in the roadway.

The seat belt protected Dad, and the crates protected me.

Dad immediately asked if I was okay, and then we both noticed the driver was not there—his door was open. I climbed forward, stepped onto the driver's seat, and was about to jump outside when I saw Costache lying right outside the door, his head a bloody mess, his eyes unblinking. I retreated and collided into Dad.

What I had seen was horrific. Dad's door was jammed shut, so he climbed out the driver's door, stepping carefully over Costache's lifeless body. With Dad's help and encouragement, I crawled back to the door and jumped out to the pavement. Dad hurried me to the side of the road, but if he was trying to shield me, it was too late. He could not erase what I had witnessed.

Costache was dead. There was nothing Dad or I could do. People who had rushed from their vehicles now stopped on both sides of the accident, then froze when they saw the lifeless body contorted in the mayhem. I trembled from the shock. Dad pulled me tight, his arm across my shoulders.

———

The police arrived. They closed the street and taped off the fatality scene.

We stood at the curb, numbly observing the carnage scattered on the road. Busted slats of wood, twisted metal, and broken glass were strewn on a sea of crushed tomatoes. The driver of the other vehicle was miraculously not seriously hurt, though the hood of his car had peeled off and the engine block was badly damaged. It was a miracle that Dad and I had only a few scratches.

When the ambulance arrived, Dad turned me to face him, resting a hand on each shoulder. "Will you be okay staying here if I can get permission to ride in the ambulance alongside Costache's body?" he asked. "I need to accompany him to the hospital."

I nodded, but my lips did not move.

"I won't be gone long."

Dad explained that he wanted to get copies of Costache's death certificate and hospital records. It would be his responsibility to inform Costache's widow and children.

I could sense Dad was more worried about me than his words revealed. I would be alone in this unfamiliar city, but he continued to reassure me that I would be safe with the police present on the scene and all the necessary activity to clean up the roadway.

The paramedics hesitated, but realized our plight. Far from home, we had no one nearby to call, and now no vehicle to drive.

My father looked at me for one more nod of assurance. I wanted to be brave, but I was frightened. I confirmed I'd be okay as I watched them load Costache's sheet-covered body, lying on a gurney. The doors closed and the ambulance pulled away.

I sat on the curb while the police finished their reports and a wrecker service arrived to clean up the mess. The mountain air was chilly and the curb cold. I thought about retrieving the blanket from inside the ARO 243 before the wrecker hauled it away, but that would mean I would have to step over the spot on the pavement where Costache had lain.

I did not move. I stared at the tomato juice flowing to the roadside gutter. I was dazed, still trying to rationalize what had just happened. I was only fifteen years old. I had almost stepped on a corpse. I had been to funerals and understood the finality of death, but this was unexpected and so sudden. *Did Costache have family? Did he have a son?* I felt alone, and I wished I were home.

———

In about forty-five minutes, a car pulled up to where I was sitting on the roadside curb, and Dad stepped out of the passenger door.

"Thanks, again, for the ride." Dad nodded to the driver and gently pressed the door shut.

I rose to stand beside him. "Who was that?" I asked.

"A nice man I met at the hospital. He offered to give me a ride. How are you doing?"

I shrugged. I was safe but sullen.

"I'm proud of you," he said.

The two of us watched in silence as the towing crew righted the trailer and pushed it clear of the roadway. The ARO 243 was then winched onto the towing truck. Both driver-side tires were blown, punctured by jagged metal.

The vehicle was hauled to an auto body shop, on the same road two miles back. Dad and I arrived on foot before the towing crew returned the second time with the trailer.

We didn't know what should or would be done with the wrecked metal. Costache's widow would need to make this decision in the future. They probably didn't have insurance, and there wasn't much left worth restoring.

The towing crew secured the vehicle and trailer in a fenced lot on the left side of the auto body shop. Dad informed the shop owner that he was welcome to salvage any of the tomatoes and distribute to friends and family. All he asked was that the wooden crates be kept and stacked for later pickup when we would pass this way again.

There were no cell phones and still no phone at the Cismigiu farm, but one of our neighbors now had a home phone, so Dad called them to relay a message to Mom about the accident. He stressed that they tell her that her husband and son were unharmed and returning by train. He did not mention Costache. This was a message he needed to deliver in person.

We took the southbound train back home. The train seemed fuller than normal, and we had to share a passenger compartment with others. Our travel companions were not in a talkative mood, which suited us just fine. The other travelers were engrossed in their own worlds—reading, staring blankly in front of them, or sleeping. I sat next to my father on the backward-facing bench, our two heads cocked sideways, staring out the window, our minds rewinding the fateful turn of events as the countryside rolled past us.

The train stopped at each station, which made for a time-consuming journey. We arrived at the Iveşti station at five in the morning the following day with me fast asleep leaning on Dad's arm. We walked home and stepped through the main gate as the sun announced the dawn of a new day.

Mom was waiting on the front porch, and she came running toward us as we arrived. She had not slept since receiving the message about our wreck.

Dad held her as Mom wrapped one arm around his neck and locked my fingers in the palm of her other hand. In almost a whisper Dad relayed the details of our journey, the accident, and the death of Costache.

The three of us retreated inside to the kitchen. Mom started pulling food from the refrigerator. Dad stepped behind her and reached over her shoulder to close the refrigerator door. He gently turned her to face him. He wrapped his muscular arms around her waist and drew her close.

"I have to break the news to Costache's wife," he said, closing his eyes. He kissed Mom's forehead, turned to look at me for a serious moment, then walked to the front door and out into the morning air.

Mom and I stood on the front porch as Dad stepped onto the road and began his walk to town.

36

Avoidance

~ Summer 1987 ~

WE hired another driver right away. Many were willing to make extra money, and Dad was willing to pay.

The abrupt and sorrowful ending to the first attempt of transporting to market by road versus rail did not dampen Dad's determination to try again. The tragedy was sobering, but the reality was that we needed this method to be successful. It was much easier with potentially a faster turnaround. The train ride took a toll on our bodies and was wearisome because of all the stops and tight connections. The best thing to do when bucked from a horse is to climb back on.

Dumitru, a retired construction worker my father knew, became our new transportation partner. He did odd jobs part-time and hauled for hire, a perfect match for our needs. He had the time to be flexible, and his equipment was road ready.

It was not surprising that his vehicle was also an ARO 243, as the automotive market in Romania did not have the variety one might expect. There were no 4×4 pickup trucks. The ARO was the most common utility vehicle—maybe the only utility vehicle—but it did come in two styles: two-door and four-door.

Dumitru had a name befitting what we desperately needed from him, "son of the right hand." He had to be an extra helping hand, not just the chauffeur. Hard labor had honed his strength and stamina, and his physical condition disguised his age.

Dad mapped out the same route we had traveled on the fateful first road trip to Vatra Dornei, and this became the road most traveled. I told myself there was no reason to be superstitious, but on each trip, I never felt safe until we passed the point where carvings from the overturned vehicle and trailer were furrowed in the pavement and memories of the horrible accident were forever etched in my mind.

This particular market promised potential, cradled in the rugged north-central Romanian mountainside, thirty-odd miles from where the Ukraine border depresses a knuckle into the Romanian landscape. The beauty of the land had been preserved, maybe due to its remoteness from the bureaucrats in Bucharest. Even the National Coat of Arms of the RSR (Socialist Republic of Romania) from 1965 to 1989 featured a depiction of the untamed nature of the Carpathian Mountains and dense population of forestry found in this area.

The final approach into Vatra Dornei on Highway A17 is picturesque, as the winding two-lane road hugs the Bistrița River. The richness of life climbs up the mountain slopes from the river on either side, dotted with layered green pasture and filling the senses with each breath of fresh mountain air. I never tired of looking at the mountains, every shadow blanketing a ravine beckoning for exploration.

Vatra Dornei was also a resort city. There were natural water springs nearby, frequented by those seeking health benefits, so there were many good hotels, mountain villas, and tourists in the area.

Health-minded tourists and city dwellers have a craving and high expectation for food quality, so our organic tomatoes were popular with both hotel and home chefs. We paid repeat visits to this city because of market demand and established relationships. But this market was the furthest away from the farm, and bribing our way through checkpoints got increasingly difficult through the years.

It was the challenge of delivery that increased. It was tough to gauge which was harder to deal with—the regular police officer who liked to up the ante or a new duty officer who had never encountered this trio and trailer before.

With the new driver and trailer, Dad had new ideas. Avoiding checkpoints was tempting, and Dad was never afraid to try a bold idea. Our nighttime travels worked to our advantage from a visual perspective when attempting off-road maneuvers but added an eerie aspect to the drama.

———

"Turn here!" Dad's shout startled me awake and broke the nighttime quiet.

Maybe he had it planned from the start, or maybe it was a sixth sense felt when approaching one of the more difficult checkpoints this particular night. Dumitru braked fast enough to thrust me forward onto the console but not jackknife the trailer.

"Do you know where this road goes?" He did not have time to wait for Dad's answer before completing the turn. The headlights illuminated a dirt road etched in a forest with tire tracks of vehicles much larger than our own.

"Someone told me about this," Dad answered. "It leads to an oil well. They said it should angle and intersect with the main road several miles north of where we normally turn to get on it. They have never driven it that far, but they said the oil well is just a few miles ahead."

There were no turnarounds carved in the tree-lined dirt path, and for the most part, it was not wide enough for two vehicles to pass side-by-side. Those who used and traveled this access to the oil well did not expect to navigate traffic. We wound our way with headlights reflecting side-to-side off tree trunks, which warned where the path edge ended.

At the bottom of the ravine was a cut clearing where we saw several old trucks and work rigs parked at random, a side-walled trailer most likely used as sleeping quarters, and a few people working. There were fewer people visible than vehicles, so we assumed the others were inside the trailer sleeping, as the windows were dark.

We crept through the maze of work vehicles and scattered equipment, positioned without thought to our passage. The oil rig workers stopped in place and turned to watch the surprising spectacle.

Dad raised his hand in the open side window to signal a friendly gesture, one that said, *Never mind us; we are just passing through.* A few workers tipped a hand upward with quizzical looks on their faces that said, *Where are you coming from, and where are you going?*

The road up the opposite side of the ravine was poured concrete, not loose gravel. Dumitru and Dad contemplated the reasoning for this and concluded that the grade was steeper and the concrete surface was probably an attempt to prevent erosion. The sheen on the surface was evidence that a rain shower had passed through earlier in the evening. The oil rig workers were out of sight, and we were back in the tunnel of trees.

Suddenly, the rear tires of the ARO lost traction, spinning freely. Dumitru kept the engine revved and allowed the tires to spin, hoping the momentum of our forward motion might push our weight upward enough to find dry spots to grip. However, the opposite happened.

The ARO was not designed for hauling such heavy loads, even on dry flat pavement. The additional weight of tomato crates packed inside helped distribute the weight over wheels, but even on dry, flat ground, the trailer weight had a tendency to push down the back bumper and lift the weight off the vehicle's front wheels.

The incline made it worse. We slipped backward. Dumitru tried to steer using his side-window mirrors. The rearview mirror was useless with all the tomato crates stacked to the ceiling.

"Cuța—lean back!"

Dumitru tried to glimpse the reflections from the brake lights off the roadway, but in the darkness, the best alignment reference came from our vehicle headlights shining up the hill in front of us. We were not aligned in the center of the roadway. Dumitru cranked the steering wheel sharply to one side, jackknifing the trailer to wedge it from slipping any further into the ditch.

"You stay behind the wheel," Dad commanded as he scrambled out his passenger door. "I will run back to get help."

We were at a complete stop. Dumitru's fingers clasped the steering wheel, his knuckles pure white. I did not fear any immediate danger, and it was not my place to speak up and suggest he loosen his death grip. We were probably thinking the same thought: *How are we going to get out of here?*

Dumitru and I stared out the front window. Our vehicle rested at an odd angle, so there wasn't much to look at, except for our headlights spotlighting the trees lining the opposite side of the roadway. I was curious how the trailer looked in its jackknifed position, but I had that "tunnel vision" effect from my tomato-crated cubbyhole, so I leaned back, rested my head against a slat, and stared blankly at the ghostly tree trunks standing at attention.

––––––

We heard the whining engine of an approaching vehicle. Dad had talked a worker into helping, and they were coming up the hillside in an oil rig. I wondered if they planned to push or pull us. It was not apparent to me how they might do either, but the commercial truck barely squeezed by, hooked a chain to our front bumper, and pulled us to the top of the hill.

The driver would not accept cash payment for his towing service, but he accepted a bag full of tomatoes. He flashed a smile and offered to assist us anytime we needed help in the future, but I felt pretty sure that Dad would not attempt this particular shortcut again, at least not if there was any chance of a damp roadway.

––––––

On a later trip to a different city market, we attempted an off-road maneuver to avoid another troublesome checkpoint, but it seemed more trouble than it was worth.

We were returning home when daylight still afforded visibility, and Dad noticed a set of tracks angling off the road a few miles prior to the checkpoint intersection where we turned. He was not worried about the checkpoint with an empty trailer in tow; in fact, we were rarely asked by the police to pull over on the return trip.

The tire tracks meandered through a field, disappearing over a distant rise in the landscape. Dad knew woods and a small creek bordered the terrain, so he was confident where the tire tracks might lead.

When we turned at the checkpoint intersection after being waved on without incident, Dad asked Dumitru to drive slower while he studied the landscape for evidence of the two-track exit. He spotted his answer several miles down the road. It was an impressive find, as the tracks were practically hidden by overgrown grass, less traveled on this end.

On our next trip to the same market, with our usual full load of crated tomatoes on the trailer and packed inside the ARO 243 surrounding my head, Dad asked Dumitru to take the two tracks to avoid the checkpoint. Dumitru did not protest, but wrinkles of caution streaked his forehead.

Luckily, there was no traffic in sight as Dumitru urged the ARO 243 along the two tracks into the darkness. The dry dirt puffed and twigs snapped under the tires as we entered the unknown.

"Are you sure where this path will exit?" Dumitru looked for reassurance. He knew what we all knew, that we had seen two tracks drift off the other road and had seen this particular set of two tracks, assuming they were connected.

"Nothing is for certain, but I am confident," answered Dad. He always spoke calmly when tensions were at their peak. "Drive slowly and be prepared to stop if we see anything lying in the tracks. Whoever drove this path repeatedly over time was surely trying to do the same as we are—looking for the easiest way from point A to B. I doubt these tracks will cross the creek."

We inched along, all three of us leaning forward, with our eyes glued to the tire tracks as the headlights snaked through what appeared to be perennial ryegrass. At least a mile or two rolled under our tires.

Dad was counting on this path cutting off the corner to avoid the checkpoint at the intersection where we would have turned north. A straight line drawn from where we entered the byway to where we hoped we would intersect the main road might have been four or five miles. But this path meandered, and it felt like we might have snaked in circles.

MARK LEE MYERS

Dad and I yelled, "Stop! Watch out!" as Dumitru slammed on the brakes. The front tires bottomed out nearly up to the axle in the rain-washed gully. Dumitru glanced at Dad with *What now?* written on his face.

"Put it in park, and let's get out and take a look," Dad told him.

I climbed out over the console and exited behind Dad. The headlights pointed downward at a sharp angle, only illuminating a short distance. The gully was not wide across, but it extended out from both sides of the vehicle, dissolving into the darkness.

"I think the trailer hitch will be stuck in the ground if we continue forward," Dumitru observed, studying the odd angle of the ARO 243 with its front tires already submerged in the gully.

"Probably so," Dad agreed.

Both men analyzed the situation, and I looked from Dad to Dumitru and back again. The stars were bright, so at least there was no fear of more rain running down this gulley tonight. It was obvious we could back out and probably turn around in the pasture without too much difficulty and head back the way we had come. To me, that was most logical, so I was surprised when Dad said otherwise.

"If we unload the tomato crates from the front of the trailer and a few from the rear of the vehicle, I think that will change the angle of the hitch enough to keep from hitting the ground when the rear tires drop into the gully. Nicolae and I can stand on the rear of the trailer for a little extra weight to raise the front end."

Unloading tomato crates in the dark of night in the middle of a pasture was not what I had dreamt of doing, but Dad did not offer the idea for debate. He was already in motion, untying the rope that had held down the crates on the front of the trailer. I think Dumitru would have voted with me to back out, turn around, and retrace the two tracks that had led us here, but there was no sense in wasting time or effort disputing Dad's plan.

Dad suggested carrying the crates to the other side of the gully and stacking them out of the way while there was glow enough from the headlights. After we pulled forward, and if we could get the trailer to the other side, it would be harder to carry the crates across the gully without stumbling in the darkness.

One by one, and I was counting, we unloaded the front half of the trailer and then the back half of the vehicle. I focused on the task without thinking too much about handling all the crates again if we ever made it to market.

"Pull ahead slowly. Nicolae and I will stand on the trailer bumper. We don't want the hitch to dig in deep and get stuck in the ground or bend something."

"I hope I have enough traction to first pull the front tires out," Dumitru said.

"Okay. We will stay off until you get the front tires out, but then stop and wait for us to climb on."

Dumitru got in the driver's seat, and Dad and I got out of the way. He shifted into low gear. With a little encouragement revving the engine, the front tires rolled right up and out the other side.

"Whoa!" I think Dad forgot he was not commanding Simi. Dumitru stopped for us to climb on the trailer bumper, Dad shouted that we were in place, and Dumitru crept forward. The vehicle rear tires slid into the gully.

Dumitru shouted from his open window. "Can you see if the hitch hit the ground?"

"Stay put," Dad instructed me. He ran forward, and the glow from the brake lights was enough to examine the hitch. "It is barely touching the dirt. Let me climb back on the rear of the trailer. I think you will be fine. We'll jump off after you pull to the other side."

The ARO rear tires rolled up and out without difficulty, and we jumped off the trailer bumper as Dumitru continued to pull forward.

"I'll drop the trailer tires into the gully and stop again," Dumitru called out.

The trailer springs creaked as the tires settled into the hole, and Dad yelled, "All clear!"

The ARO strained a little harder with the weight of the tomato crates loaded behind the trailer wheels, so Dumitru eased on the gas, allowing the trailer to rock backward, and then accelerated enough to bump up out of the hole.

We spoke not a word, but we all smiled with relief.

Dumitru put the vehicle in park, and we all reloaded and secured the crates. Dad made one last check to ensure no tomato crate was left in the grass.

We continued driving on full alert. I kept fingers crossed on both my hands for double good luck, and it must have helped, as we never found another obstacle to navigate. The two tracks on this side of the gully were more heavily traveled, and there were tracks that veered from the main, but we stuck with the well-worn ones.

Dumitru and Dad concentrated on where the headlights bumped and turned, so I was the first to see the hope of success.

I shouted, "There is the main road!"

The lights of a moving car heading southbound were visible across the field. I wondered if I was the only one hoping it was not a police car.

When we edged up and onto the main road, we were lucky to see no other travelers approaching. The two-track escapade had spared us a checkpoint, but we had lost time. Dad did not comment, but I felt this might be the first time we arrived late to market.

It was not my decision, but I did venture to guess. We might use the two-track path again, but I doubted we would take the turnoff in the rain. I also hoped Dad would think of an ingenious way to get across the gully without requiring the unloading and reloading.

We had been very lucky for many years, but luck doesn't last forever.

37

Sweetening the Pot

~ Summer 1987 ~

DAD discovered troves of treasure chests full of bribe paraphernalia. The treasure chests were the trunks of tourist vehicles parked in the scattered rest stops along Highway E85.

During one of our nighttime transports, we pulled into a rest stop that surprisingly had room for our vehicle and trailer. We seldom stopped in these roadside pull-offs; usually there was not enough room for our double-length transport trolley. Dumitru pulled in for a quick check of his trailer, and Dad and I got out to stretch our legs.

Many of the travelers were foreigners heading for the Black Sea, with little Fiat cars pulling little trailers. The ones we met this night were from Poland. They had stopped for a rest as well, but their main purpose was to open their trunks and trailers to display their reservoir of contraband for sale.

This was how they subsidized or completely paid for their vacation. Their trunk store contained jeans, gold chains, Kent cigarettes, coffee beans, chewing gum, candy, LaCoste shirts, and a variety of other items not readily found in Romanian stores. I never saw my father pass up a good deal, and he was not afraid of buying supplies on the black market.

Dad saw an opportunity, and Dumitru and I thought he had lost his mind. He did not give us advance warning of his long-term intentions.

He started buying like an alcoholic bingeing at an open bar. He bought twenty cartons of cigarettes and several kilos of coffee. When I watched him negotiate the inclusion of candy and chewing gum, I changed my opinion in favor of his actions. The vacationers were interested in cash, but Dad insisted they accept a few tomato crates in the trade to make room inside our vehicle for the additional cargo he had purchased.

When we pulled back onto the northbound lane of E85, Dad explained that what he had done was purchase better bribes. It made perfect sense.

I should have known better than to wonder if Dad was taking up smoking. Cigarettes were a powerful bribe. Even police, who did not smoke, wanted cigarettes, but only the Kent brand. Cigarettes all smelled the same to me but maybe Kents were the status brand. Police also needed the ability to negotiate, so a few extra packs of cigarettes often were worth more than cash. Barter and bribery were the way of life.

Dad also explained his assumption, which later proved true, that a single bag of foreign coffee would open doors and hearts.

––––––––

The marketing law of supply and demand was artificially altered throughout Romania at this time. There was high demand for goods and services, but the government kept the supply low.

Location, location, location is the secret to a successful real estate deal. A strategically located booth to display goods for sale and provide maximum exposure to passers-by was as crucial as a billboard positioned on a prime pinnacle or a neon sign at a busy intersection. Whenever there was uncertainty regarding the availability of a better booth locale, Dad would present a bag of coffee to the market manager. This gesture spoke a language all its own and earned us one of the best booths in the market.

Even blue jeans were hard to come by and considered contraband. I only had known them sold on the black market. We traveled across the county at least once a year to a big open-air market in the city of Timisoara to buy difficult-to-find products, such as jeans, smuggled in from Hungary. A pair of jeans might cost half of a common laborer's monthly salary.

Jeans cost several hundred *lei*, depending on the brand name. A monthly salary for unskilled labor averaged twelve hundred *lei*. A good monthly salary for skilled labor ranged from two to three thousand *lei*. One cannot simply equate that salary to one in a different country at that time. More important was the buying power of the money. People had plenty of money, but there was little to buy.

On our first encounter with a Fiat trunk sale, Dad did not have enough extra cash to purchase jeans. But he always traveled with additional cash after discovering these roadside "shopping malls."

———

As we drove northbound into the night after our first roadside shopping experience, I felt proud of my father's ingenuity and sensed the positive impact these alternative bribes might have to ease our tomato transport. I didn't care for the coffee or cigarettes, but I had purely selfish thoughts of Dad's intentions for the candy and chewing gum. I understood why Dad did not want to give me a sugar high when it was already late; we had miles to go before daybreak. But I think I would've gotten more rest if he had given me a piece or two to satisfy my craving. As I leaned my head against the wooden crate and closed my eyes, I thought of the candy rather than falling asleep.

38

Double or Nothing

~ Winter 1987 ~

DAD was not a gambler, but he loved to buy at a bargain and sell at a profit.

The pig slaughter at Christmastime is one example of my father's approach to purchasing. Pigs were sold for about half price near mountain towns, which not only saved money but saved the time and trouble of caring for the pig all year long. And if he was going to transport one pig, he might as well buy in quantity.

Dad always found neighbors, friends, and relatives who desired fattened pigs for the holidays. They agreed to buy from him for more than the current mountain market price, but still at a bargain compared to the local cost.

Dad hired a driver to take him to the mountains a week before Christmas. Transporting tons of tomatoes by rail had already proved challenging, so attempting to conceal a bunch of squealing pigs on a moving train was out of the question. It was not a crime to own pigs, nor a crime to transport them across a county line, but the parcel boxcar and the passenger train compartment could not be used as a temporary pigpen.

The checkpoints were easier to navigate during the colder months, as the police were lazier and stopped fewer vehicles. Police focused more on summer tomatoes, especially in the quantity we hauled to market. They were not concerned was about someone making a single trade with pigs for the purpose of feeding their family.

Dad bought four pigs, each weighing about two hundred kilos. He sold three pigs for a profit that covered the cost of the one he kept.

———

Somewhere along the line, Dad also realized the magic of turning corn into potatoes.

The Siret River Valley soil and weather promoted plentiful corn production, but the average warm air temperature and the limited land each family was permitted to own hindered growing potatoes in abundance.

This was not true of the higher elevation and mountainous conditions in other parts of Romania. With cooler air and more land available per person, those areas were ideal for growing potatoes.

It was also a factor that rural, mountainous regions were of greater distance from Bucharest, and therefore less hindered by any communist "outreach" program that might try to control production quotas. The government allowed these landowners more acreage for cattle grazing, which allowed for larger gardens and fields as well.

Our family focus was on the full-scale production of our cash crop, so we grew tomatoes but no potatoes on our property. Like most brainstorms of our father, another entrepreneurial opportunity was born.

Dad loved potatoes, and he realized that many other Siret River Valley folks liked them also. Late in the fall season, when autumn leaves blushed tones of yellow and red, and the last of our tomatoes had been harvested, Dad rounded the radius of the nearby communities with horse and wagon to purchase his initial bartering stock of corn. He collected the corn and stored it in gunnysacks until he hired a driver with a vehicle to transport him and his corn to a mountain town where the bartering began.

Dad used the two-for-one method: one kilo of his product for two of another. By day's end, he came home with more gunnysacks than when he had started, all full of potatoes.

This was only round one.

Dad had a following of customers who came knocking on our front door asking for potatoes. He often asked for corn in exchange, rather than cash.

He hauled his potatoes along with a portable scale to neighboring towns and established his presence on a street corner. One person would spread the news, and folks came with pushcarts full of corn. In thirty minutes, fifty people stood in line, willing and ready to trade two-for-one.

A person might imagine that bartering was our dad's hobby, to keep himself busy in the wintertime, but we children had a different view. Dad always enlisted—actually, insisted on—our help.

We loved eating potatoes, but we could have done with a few less or even given them up completely. Our dad's bartering genius meant a year-round work schedule: a doubling of our duties.

39

Easy Does It

I ADVANCED to eleventh grade as I turned seventeen. When my sister graduated the previous year, she moved back home to look for work, and she found more than she was looking for. She met her fiancé. The same year, my brother enlisted in the military. This left me alone in the big city of Bacău when I had not yet learned self-discipline.

School years can be tough, even when a student knows many kids from the community. Most kids in this technical high school were local residents who already knew each other, but I knew no one in this city far from home. That is, until I met Radu in eleventh grade. I think I intrigued him by being the only farm kid—a real live country boy.

He invited me to his home after school one day to study together, but the aroma drifting from the kitchen as his mother prepared supper distracted me from homework. I was thrilled when his mother invited me to stay and eat. My mother would have been horrified by my imposition.

Radu's mother treated me like her own son and became my surrogate mom. She was not as intrigued at my being a country boy as she was because I was living alone so far from home. She never probed into my family history; it was only important that I show up on time when she invited me for a meal.

Radu's mother worked at a movie theater. In our hometown, the movie theater was a nondescript city hall building, overflowing with more paying patrons than available seats. In larger Romanian cities like Bacău, movie theaters were located in beautiful, ornately decorated buildings. The movies in larger cities were better quality, but there still was only one movie selection per day, and it played repeatedly.

Radu and I went to the movie theater after school, and his mother let us in for free. We watched the one movie three times, waiting for his mother to get off work. After the last showing, she gave us the job of cleaning the theater.

This form of entertainment might have been low cost, but it came at the expense of my educational progress. Radu's mother probably quizzed him to confirm completion of his homework prior to bedtime, but I had no one at my apartment checking on my schoolwork.

The movies after school should have either satisfied my teenage cinema cravings or triggered brain burnout. It was a diversion from homework, and I could sleep through the third showing if the film was boring. My real test of endurance was an all-night, seven-feature movie marathon.

Travelers abroad smuggled in VCRs and videos: Rambo, Chuck Norris, Jackie Chan, Bruce Lee (any karate or action film)—the good stuff. Some entrepreneur would schedule a movie night in their apartment and charge twenty-five *lei* to watch seven movies. News of the movie madhouse surfaced by word of mouth.

We arrived at the stated address, and if the host did not already know us, we mentioned a code word or talked our way into the party. There might be twenty people inside when the lights dimmed and the VCR started. Kids sat on couches, chairs, and floor. The seven movies played back-to-back all night long.

The immersion of imagery left me exhausted and red-eyed, but I always asked when the next video shipment was coming and persuaded the host to invite me again.

Just before sunrise, most people walked home, or in my case, back across the city to my apartment. No bus or public transportation ran at that time of morning. It might take me two hours to walk home depending on how far across the city the movie house was located.

We took our homework responsibility more seriously on days we did not visit the movie theater. At least, we had good intentions.

We started by walking with our backpacks and books to the library for a quiet place to study. The library building, like many of the old structures, was also ornately beautiful. Being a country boy, I marveled at the architecture in the big cities.

After fifteen to twenty minutes of study, we were bored silly. Talking was discouraged in the library, but we knew how to read each other's minds and body language. One frown, shoulder shrug, and head nod was all it took. Moments later, we departed.

Our next stop was a pastry café. It was the place to be and be seen, very similar to the county fair in my parents' day. The café had two expansive floors and offered an elaborate variety of cheesecakes, cookies, tarts, and a selection of coffees and teas. We purchased a pastry and drink and then hung out for hours. This was where school-age kids socialized and where boys met girls.

My grades suffered, but my social life flourished. I feared and respected my parents, so I never told them the real story. I don't consider myself lazy or a procrastinator, especially now in my adult life, but an unsupervised young man in his junior and senior years of high school does not make the most mature decisions. I did enough to get by but not enough to excel.

40

Sinking Feeling

~ Fall 1988 ~

WE persevered. But others found it more difficult to cope with government oppression. Although it was not something ever printed in a state-sponsored newspaper or discussed on the daily television propaganda, stories of defections were common. We cheered those who succeeded and felt sympathy for those who were unfortunate.

There were a variety of escape routes. The remote ones seemed more likely for success, but those had extra elements of danger. We heard of attempts to swim across the Danube River into Yugoslavia. Some defectors, confused in the nighttime darkness and circling currents, mistakenly ended up returning to the Romanian shore and were apprehended by the police or exposed by other Romanians.

It hit close to home when I learned that a neighbor had attempted to find freedom outside Romania. Mom bore the news when she came to visit me in Bacău.

I felt stunned. Constantin was five years older than my brother; he and I were not close friends. But I remembered his smile. He was always smiling. And he had moved to the western part of our country to live and work. My mind raced to remember the last time I had seen him.

"When did Constantin attempt it?" I asked.

"His parents are not sure of the exact day, but it had to have been about two weeks ago. He didn't show up for work, and his employer contacted the authorities."

That made sense. The military police in that part of the country specialized in border control and were on alert for defectors to Yugoslavia. Most of the neighboring countries didn't have much more freedom to offer than our own, but Yugoslavia assisted defectors, making it an attractive escape route.

"Did his parents get a phone call?"

"Worse than that. The police showed up at their home."

I interrupted. "Did they get into trouble?" My heart was beating fast. Memories echoed of the police stomping onto our front porch. No personal, physical harm had been done, but the outcome of each visit had etched an emotional scar.

"She couldn't tell me much, but I don't think they did."

The police had asked his parents what their son might have said, either about his intentions to leave or derogatory feelings about communism. His parents had not known about his intentions to defect, and they for sure would not have revealed any deep-seated ill feelings.

"I do know this, Constantin was a good young man." Mom's voice choked, and she paused. I felt a lump in my throat as well.

Mom brushed a tear from her cheek and continued. "He surely felt desperation. It would have been painful for him not to be able to say, 'Goodbye,' but his reasoning for not doing so is obvious." Constantin, like so many defectors, would have been torn between family and breaking free from government oppression.

I nodded in agreement.

Mom had been staring at nothing in particular, but now, her eyes penetrated and held my gaze. "Nicolae …," she said. Moisture swelled at the corners of her eyes. I felt the urge to reach out and try to stop the tear, but one burst through her eyelash and streaked down her cheek before I could extend my finger to touch it.

I reached out and cradled her clasped hands in mine. My parents had sacrificed so much to provide a taste of freedom—freedom from communist oppression. I had never thought of defecting, but I had dreamt of what complete freedom might be like.

"Mom, all I want to do is make you proud. You and Dad have done more than I can fully appreciate. I love Romania, especially the old Romania I hear about. I pray that Romania may one day be free again. But I do dream of traveling the world. I know how much you are afraid of swimming, so I'll promise to go by boat or plane."

I grinned. Mom raised her eyebrows and feigned a smile.

"That's most likely what Constantin did," Mom said.

"What? Swim?" I gasped. "Have they heard from him?"

"No. But Yugoslavia was most likely his destination, and swimming might have been the safest way for him to attempt escape."

The Danube River was the border with Yugoslavia. There were few bridges and little chance that Constantin would have encountered a border-check station. We learned the story of his attempt some time later.

———

CONSTANTIN perched near the riverbank, concealed from view, but with a good field of vision from between the outcrop of dense vegetation. He had enough water and food to last two more days, if necessary. He was patient. This was a risk with the highest stakes. He was attempting to defect to Yugoslavia by swimming across the Danube River. He would get only one chance.

Constantin had been at the riverbank for two days, observing the pattern of the police patrol boats. The boats, especially at night, focused on the narrowest points between both shores.

He crouched on the Romanian side. The other shore might appear, to the natural eye, quite similar to where he was hidden, but it was the soil of freedom. It looked vastly different from his angle of decision. Yugoslavia allowed defectors to choose among three asylum countries. America was his first choice. America was his only choice.

Constantin shifted his weight, careful to ensure he did not move even a leaf or snap one twig. There was no such thing as being too cautious.

The police in the patrol boats were trained to watch for defectors. It was assumed that defectors were poised to take the chance, and the police were rewarded handsomely if they caught such a criminal.

Few, if any, would dare swim the river in the daylight, so the patrol was less focused on the water but rather scanning the shoreline for a reflective sparkle from a button or the contrast of coloring from the clothes of any waiting fugitive. Constantin had dressed appropriately. He would remain camouflaged even if a patrol boat were to glide by.

Tonight.

Constantin felt comfortable with his decision. The narrow passage was most risky because of the frequency of patrol boats and searchlights that swarmed these waters. Only a fool would try to swim the swift current at its widest point, so the police boats navigated those parts much less frequently on night patrol. Constantin smiled to himself; the smile of a fool.

Darkness thickened, and the heavens seemed to nod approval for his passage—the moon was hiding its face, and the stars were veiled in a faint fog cover. In the distance, patrol boats crisscrossed the river with floodlights probing for victims.

Constantin drank his remaining fresh water supply and finished his crust of bread. There was no convenient way to take his water container with him, and the food would dissolve in his pockets. He needed free hands during the long swim for freedom.

With mixed emotions, Constantin slithered to the shoreline, sliding into the water like the snakes he hoped were not nearby. He dragged a small log with him as a life preserver.

His foot pushed off, and the water caressed and carried his body forward. Despite an instant feeling of freedom, an emptiness hovered in his Romanian heart. His beautiful country and heritage had been robbed by a greedy government.

He cut the negativity anchor and let it sink behind him. His mind needed to be clear. As he stroked with his free palm and propelled forward with his feet, the driftwood floated out into the blackened surge.

The fog thickened as the night chilled. The stars stopped blinking on the river surface. Constantin's navigation was now dependent on his internal compass, and it was swirling in the river current, disoriented.

He lost track of time. His wooden life preserver hindered his progress. He suspected he had reached the middle as the river flow felt swifter, but this was not to his advantage. The log had caught the river rush like a sail catches the wind. He was moving faster but downstream in the wrong direction.

Even though heavy fog hovered over the water, helping to conceal his bobbing body, Constantin knew he would be at risk of being discovered if he continued to drift downstream to where the river narrowed.

He had no other choice. He let go of the driftwood and started kicking in the direction perpendicular to his wooden life preserver, which now drifted out of reach.

He had never swum this far with or without his clothes on, and the weight of his clothing restricted his movements, pulling him downward. He thought about undressing. He was not afraid of having nothing to wear on the opposite shore but that he didn't have enough strength to tread water while trying to discard his garments. So he kept swimming fully clothed.

Out of breath. No strength. Constantin was not a quitter, but he had to quit. It was not a mental choice but a physical demand. He could go no further.

His face was obviously water soaked, but he felt tears stream down his cheeks. He tried to kick one last time, but his water-clogged pants and shoes restricted movement. He was settling upright. He flung his arms in one last attempt to keep his head above water.

41

Convicted Felon

~ Spring 1989 ~

A STORM was brewing.

My father did not obey every law, and those he broke were for the purpose of sustaining life. I am not talking about sensible laws, such as vehicle speed limits or criminal acts against humanity, but rather ridiculous laws, such as citizens not being permitted to butcher their own cow.

Citizens were allowed to own a pig and slaughter it for their personal use, but it was prohibited for a citizen to butcher their own cow. It was a felony punishable by jail time.

To someone growing up in a free society, it might seem bizarre that the Romanian government attempted to control livestock by census counts. It was strange, but true.

I remember at a young age asking Dad for the short explanation, but he was always generous with his educational handouts.

"The government mandates that cows must be sold at a slaughterhouse, where they regulate the price per kilo well under market value, and then export it at or above market value. There is no consideration for citizens making a profit or simply providing protein for their families. The objective is elimination of national debt and preservation of presidential pride on the world stage," Dad explained.

"Most things political are not designed in the best interest of those being governed. Many communist dictates are based on greed and monopolistic control. Communism discourages competition and does not breed quality, nor does its recipe for equality produce economical abundance, as there is no incentive to excel."

Teachers were paid by the government when school was not in season to conduct a census of bodies and bovines. These teachers often seemed more interested in the paycheck and less in confirming accuracy of counts. Therefore, the census was conducted more like an interview from the comforts of the kitchen table or living room chair.

The census taker would simply ask, "How many people live in this home? What are the respective age groups? Do you have cattle, and if so, how many head?"

There was rarely a search of the barn or property to confirm the supplied numbers, which allowed my father to buy a young cow, fatten him, and then proceed under the cover of darkness to slaughter the animal for food. A friendly neighbor helped Dad, and in turn, Dad helped him.

I wanted to be on the inside of the barn the night of the slaughter, but I never got that opportunity. My job was to help Mom cover every window with blankets and then walk around the barn to confirm no light leaked through any window or crack in the barn siding. By morning, the slaughter process was completed, and the cowhide was rolled up and buried with the carcass.

Mom cut the beef into small steaks, deep-fried them, and placed them into jars covered with hot grease. She stored the jars without a lid in the cool cellar, where the grease hardened to preserve the meat.

Under the cover of darkness, my father disobeyed the butchering law every springtime or summer when our meat supply from the slaughtered pig before Christmas was running low. It was a gamble, and luckily, he never got caught. But his luck would not last forever.

————

The springtime destruction of my father's tomato crop by the local police intensified each year. Their acts of harassment in the early years seemed more focused on intimidation, to weaken my father's resolve. But as the years rolled by and his resolve strengthened, the police tried to think of reasons to have him jailed. We saw this storm cloud building on the horizon, and there was no way of escaping its destruction. We tried to brace for it.

On any given year, the Communists might rule it unlawful to grow corn on family farms, and the next year corn might be approved and soybeans the outlawed contraband. I remember soybeans often being on the forbidden list. The government didn't want competition with their exports. They could control the price with controlled production.

This spring, after the police overran our newly planted tomatoes, they scattered a three-kilo package of soybean seeds in the field. It was not enough seed to plant the entire field; it was a symbolic gesture.

It was a felony to damage government property, which they considered my parents' land to be. They tempted my father to commit a violation, which would lead to a trial. The government wanted to beat him in the courts if they could not beat him with physical intimidation.

Dad consulted with friends and a professor fluent in legal matters to attract the attention and favor of the Supreme Court before replanting. His professor friend crafted a well-written *reclamatie* document that explained what the police force was perpetrating: destruction of personal property, confiscation of land, and harassment and intimidation of civilians. Included were dozens of black and white photos, which I had taken to capture the police in action.

My mother and brother hand-delivered the *reclamatie* to the courthouse in Bucharest. We were not sure the court would be sympathetic toward our plight, but we wanted to be heard.

The Romanian Constitution said one thing and the authorities did something else. The court clerks accepted the paperwork but did not allow Mom to speak with the court magistrates.

After a few weeks of waiting with no response from the higher court, Dad plowed the soil under and replanted his second wave of tomato plants. He had tried the legal route, knowing the gravity of the situation, but he could not wait any longer to replant if we expected to reap a harvest.

Similar to the time the authorities had stormed onto my grandparents' property long before I was born, looking for the hidden stash of hunting rifles, the police charged to our home a few days after this second planting. The purpose of their visit was no longer mere intimidation; they fully intended to strike where it might hurt my father most.

Dad was arrested and taken into custody, but that wasn't the worst of it. This was not the first time he had been accused and hauled into court. Monetary fines were assessed each year because the government claimed he was using their property, which they had confiscated, at least on paper, years prior. Dad kept current with his tax payments, always submitting sufficient funds to cover all his acreage, but he never paid the penalty assessed for his use of 'government' land, because the land he was farming was his own.

In times past, he had been a rock—a boulder that wouldn't budge—which confounded authorities. He had flamed the fire of freedom, a torch that the winds of previous court trials had not extinguished. But this time, my father was convicted and sentenced.

I remembered my father telling me of the vows he had made when he witnessed the brutal police raid in the driveway of his parents' home when he was young. He vowed to persevere. I had never doubted my father, but I was now old enough to understand that even he had limitations. The future was filled with uncertainties. And Mom was no longer alone in bearing the burden of fear.

To put my father behind bars or reprove with monetary punishment was not painful enough for the government's satisfaction. The court fully intended to take those actions, but first they wanted to strike one final blow that would surely hurt both Dad's heart and his harvest.

The police took Simi.

Dad argued that his prized stallion had been outright stolen! The gravity of losing Simi was intense. Beyond the fact that the great stallion could not easily be replaced, Dad had a deep bond and respect for the horse.

Simi was relocated to a government-run farm where they worked him during the day. Occasionally, they loaned him to one of our neighboring farmers. The officials knew he would pass by our front gate to and from his own farm, and this taunting drove my father crazy.

MARK LEE MYERS

42

Saving Simi

~ Summer 1989 ~

DAD saw Simi trot past our farm gate many times. One day, he saw the farmer with Simi pulling a heavy load of firewood, and Dad could no longer restrain himself. He ran outside.

"Nicolae, start taking pictures!"

Hearing the urgency in Dad's voice, I grabbed the camera and snapped a quick photograph of the horse approaching, but unfortunately, that was the end of the roll of film.

Dad rushed to the middle of the road and stood there, blocking their passage, forcing the farmer to bring Simi to an abrupt halt.

"Whoa!" the farmer shouted, pulling hard on the reins.

Dad grabbed Simi's harness so the horse would not bolt if the farmer slapped the reins. With a jerk, he yanked the reins from the farmer's hands, almost unbalancing the man from the wagon seat.

"What are you doing?" demanded the man perched on the trailer.

"I am taking my horse," Dad retorted.

"But you can't—"

"Shut up!" Dad interrupted. "You know this is my horse. You know the government stole him. You have enjoyed the pleasure of his use long enough."

Dad unhooked the traces and tug chains from the harness hames, letting them fall to the ground. Without another word, Dad stood as tall as a stocky man could and walked Simi through our front gate to the barn.

The authorities had hoped Dad would give in, but instead, Dad gave back—he counterpunched. Dad was not naive. There would be hell to pay for his bold action, but a man can tolerate only so much.

The police came within a few days and hauled Dad into court again, and although he put up a good fight and laid out a convincing story about the injustices done to him, he lost again. Simi was taken back into the State's custody, and Dad's financial debt to the government increased.

Dad's final sentence date was purposefully set by the court to be the following January so that they could watch him struggle without Simi and finally surrender to the communists' demands.

Dad worried about Simi constantly.

As the heat of summer sweltered, a friend of my father, who worked at the government farm, alerted us that the stallion was being overworked. Dad often thought aloud of possible scenarios for reclaiming his rightful ownership, but legal options had been squelched, and it seemed undeniable that Dad would serve jail time after his pending court date.

The threat of incarceration and continued harassment and intimidation did not unnerve Dad. He only was stressed about Simi's health and welfare.

"I'm going there tonight," Dad blurted at the supper table one evening.

"Going where?" Mom questioned.

"I have to see Simi. I have to make contact with him. I must see up close what condition he is in. He needs to feel my reassurance that I have not forgotten him, that I will save him at any cost!"

There could be many arguments against such a dangerous attempt in the dead of night, but none of us voiced our concerns. Dad was determined. The look in his eyes clearly said there would be no persuasion strong enough to change his mind.

MARK LEE MYERS

Dad stood in the shadows of a lone tree observing the layout of the government farm from a safe distance.

The nearby farmland stretched for miles, cultivated with a variety of crops that employed many workers during planting and harvest seasons. A main attraction of this expansive operation was the conglomerate of nearly one hundred long, single-story barns and feedlots.

This was a factory farm where animals were birthed and fattened for later transport to slaughtering houses. The majority of the barns housed animals for slaughter, but several barns stored workhorses, hay, and heavy-duty farm equipment.

There might have been a few horses among the thousands of animals awaiting their final butchered fate, but the police had no desire to kill Simi for his meat. Simi was worth more alive than dead when it came to the continued misery they could inflict on my father by separating him from his beloved stallion. This was simply a convenient place to house the horse while they waited for my father to surrender and submit to their demands.

Dad walked a crooked path to the closest barn, keeping away from the dim lights scattered sparsely on wooden poles. Finding Simi's stall would be difficult in the daylight, but Dad was not welcome at any time. The cover of darkness was his ticket to trespass.

He passed quickly between the barns, eliminating them as options for entry by the type of animal stench emanating from within. He had not seen any lights reflecting from any barn interior so far, but he remained on high alert for a chance encounter with a farmhand who might be completing late-night chores.

Dad was not aware of any security patrol. Anticipated punishment was a fairly adequate deterrent to the average citizen. Communism could be credited for more action and less talk when it came to administering discipline.

Luck had been on his side so far because he had not encountered anyone, but he might need more than luck to find Simi in the maze of concrete buildings. The soft lowing from cattle and the squeals from pigs told him Simi was not inside those buildings.

Simi had a territorial temperament, which made Dad assume the police may have housed this stallion away from other horses. There were so many barns, so many squeaky door hinges, but abandoning his search was not an option. He had to find Simi even if it required staying there all night.

He neared the building that seemed quieter than others and sensed it might be the one. It wasn't any particular smell or sound that heightened his hope, and he'd guessed wrong a few times already.

He tried the small barn door, and it was either locked or blocked from within. *Maybe I should just come back to this one later,* he first thought. And then the feeling pricked him again. *Try this one now,* the inner voice told him.

He quickened his step and glanced over his shoulder. Several yards down the back side, a second door gave way. He turned the knob and leaned his shoulder inward. Horse scent filled his nostrils as he inhaled: warm, musky, mossy with streaks of sweat. He let his sense of smell lead him toward the far end where the locked door was located.

The illumination from an outside pole light crept through the scattered windows perched high on the cement walls, outlining darkened silhouettes of equipment strewn on the floor. The building was mainly used for storage. He stepped carefully. This was not the time to chance injury. There would be no one to help him. The only people who knew he was here were too far away to help.

"Simi ... is that you, my boy?" Dad spoke softly.

He could see the outline of a horse above the railing and stall door. The animal had the height of Simi's large body, but the neck was drooped and hanging low. Lifeless. Simi would have nickered long before now if his master had approached him in the barn at home. But this *was* Simi. Dad *knew* it to be true. The once great stallion was not avoiding his master, nor had he forgotten the sound of his voice. The horse was exhausted and frail. He had not been well cared for as my father had so lovingly done.

Dad reached out and gently stroked the stallion's mane. Dad contorted his face, writhing with anger to realize how his prized stallion was starving for proper care.

Communism satisfies selfish motives at the expense of others' liberty, he thought to himself. *Even the liberty of an animal. It is the epitome of arrogance.*

"I'm going to find a way to free you." Dad leaned his head against the horse and rubbed Simi's nose. "I promise!"

43

Radical Removed

~ Winter 1989 ~

MY father told me it was commonly suspected that the Russian government put President Nicolae Ceaușescu in power in Romania in 1965. At first, Ceaușescu separated himself from hardcore Russian Communists by masquerading as a reformist. This gave a false sense of hope that freedom, to some degree, was dawning in Romania.

During the early 1970s, President Ceaușescu was widely popular because his true radical ideals were not yet evident. Even so, the administration and execution of the Ceaușescu totalitarian philosophies were more strongly enforced in particular regions of Romania. We happened to live in a rural region where this was evident.

As with any dictator whose power has been gained by coercion, President Ceaușescu had grown increasingly paranoid. His control lingered for twenty-five years, and he resorted to harsh persecution of real and imagined enemies.

The fall of communism was rampant across Europe by 1989, and Romanians were fed up with the repressive lifestyle imposed; theirs was a pride and heritage worth reclaiming.

When the Romanian national revolution started on December 16, 1989, I was in my last year of high school. Life had already been an educational experience, but nothing could compare with the events that unfolded to overthrow the Communist regime, and the immediate aftermath.

After President Ceauşescu and his wife were shot, and the Communist regime he had propped up crumbled, there was a mad dash by citizens to reclaim assets the Communists had confiscated and redistributed.

It was a chaotic and bloody debate. People made claims on their old plots of ground, but some local officials still thought that they had the power. The authorities tried to appear fair, knowing that the people had toppled a powerful regime. But there was a lot of confusion and unclaimed land due to people who had moved away or died in the years since the land had been confiscated, so authorities still tried to keep land for themselves and their cronies, arguing over ownership and pushing people around. The bureaucratic procedures to reclaim assets were too cumbersome, so impatient citizens took matters into their own hands.

In one such case, a friend of my father was killed in the scuffle over land ownership. He had chosen to side too closely with the wrong crowd. He had aligned with communism, and for his loyalty, was a recipient of their land redistribution program. But when the rightful owner rose up to reclaim the stolen asset, this man's life was cut short in a knife fight. Unfortunate deaths occurred on both sides.

For Dad, the shackles of his harassment and intimidation sprang open, and the doom of his pending court sentencing evaporated. Our relief was instantaneous, like a sudden change in barometric pressure. For years, the bureaucrats had inflicted pain. Now, they were no longer in power. My family felt a joy beyond description.

We all cried.

Dad had never feared his pending jail term, nor worried about an ever-increasing monetary fine. These were burdens that weighed heavily on the rest of the family, but all he was concerned about was saving Simi.

The day after we learned of President Ceauşescu's death, I went with Dad to the government farm where Simi had been held. Dad darted through the barn doors, and no one dared try to stop him. He ran to Simi's stall and flung the gate open with such intensity that I thought it might spring off its hinges. Not normally one to show much affection, Dad threw his arms around Simi's neck and embraced him tightly.

"We're going home, Simi," Dad whispered. "We're going home where you belong."

———

Months later, a knock came on our door. The stranger had a warm and pleasant personality and explained that a museum about communism was being opened in Bucharest. Archives of atrocities and volumes of historical data were being gathered and would be made available to the public.

The man standing at the front door was a professor of history, and he was helping to compile data from our region. He had heard of my father's reputation for fighting for liberty without violence. He hoped to extract additional information, and he tried to educate and encourage my father to research the museum archives to possibly reveal by whom our family had been persecuted.

But Dad was not interested. "I am forgiving everybody," I remember him saying. "Judgment is a jailor, and heaven knows we already have too many in bondage. People only did what they had to do to survive."

44

Liberty Lottery

~ Winter 1993 ~

GRANDPA believed the Americans would come and liberate Romania. His thoughts were a product of a war mentality ingrained by a lifetime of struggle with foreign occupation and dictatorship. He never lived to see the day, but ironically, his presumption did come true. His dream skipped one generation and by fate landed directly on me. And fate landed me in the city of Galați.

This bustling city, the largest in our home county, hugs a swooping bend in the Danube River. The Danube flows wide and deep with easy access to the Black Sea, so the water always churns with commerce. Romania's largest shipyard is located there along with the largest iron and steel plant in the country. This demands the involvement of several boat operations—tugboats, fuel tankers, icebreakers, and firefighting boats.

After the revolution, my brother returned home from his military service and got a job in Galați working as an electrician on a firefighting riverboat. After the cost and effort it had taken our dad to obtain a work permit for him, I was surprised Marin did not seek a full-time job at the military manufacturing facility in Bacău that he had once coveted.

But jobs—good ones—were hard to come by, and the one in Galați was a government job with good benefits. It was also a suitable job for students going to the university there because it allowed time for both studying and fun during the twenty-four-hour work shifts and the seventy-two hours off. It was also the same place my sister's fiancé worked, which gave him an edge with the hiring manager.

I followed in my brother's footsteps, through high school and onto my initial career path, but he is not to blame for my mistakes. I did not pass the university entrance exam on the first try either, but it was probably because I wasted much of the eleventh and twelfth grades goofing off.

After graduating high school in 1990 and then fulfilling my mandatory military duties the following year, I secured a job on the same firefighting boat. Our work schedules allowed us to live at home and commute the forty miles to the riverboat.

Our boss liked us. I would like to think it was for some prideful reason, such as intelligence, good looks, and humor, but he appreciated our trustworthiness and dependability. He was the captain, and we looked up to him with respect as our manager and mentor.

I was part of a crew responsible for extinguishing boat fires and any fires at loading docks or shoreline buildings that our onboard water cannons could reach. However, during my time on duty, I never fought one fire. I was paid to be ready. The firefighting riverboat docked in a beautiful downtown marina. Patrolling the riverbank was as relaxing as a Sunday afternoon walk in the park with the comforts of a riverboat cruise.

The extra leisure time gave me the freedom to daydream. Dreams often become obsessions, but I tried to keep mine grounded in reality. Sometimes a person works hard and long to make dreams come true, and it seems they never will, and then they meet someone who influences their direction in life.

One day, during a casual conversation with the captain, I voiced my dream to travel abroad—maybe even live outside of Romania. My heart skipped a beat when he exclaimed, "You might be lucky enough to win."

"Win what?" I said, excited but confused.

The captain told me about a newspaper article announcing a lottery-type immigration program as a result of the deepened diplomatic relationships between our new Romanian government and the United States of America. The article was not on the front page, but he recalled it being a short story in some secondary part of some newspaper. He did not remember the date or which newspaper.

The captain seemed more excited than me to find the newspaper article. He was anchored with a good life and a good wife. For him, uprooting and exploring abroad was not an option.

As a young man, he had been a sailor on a cargo ship. He described the thrill of seeing the horizon and wondering what might lay beyond it. He had seen America from the deck of a merchant ship, longing to reach out and touch it, but never had the opportunity to step ashore. He shared these stories with a dreamy nostalgia in his eyes. Maybe helping me set sail would let him live out his dream.

We rushed to the library and rummaged through stacks of newspapers looking for the news article. After several hours, we found it. The article was simply titled: "Green Card Lottery." It explained that the United States Congress had enacted a Diversity Immigrant Visa program. The lottery would allow a select few to win the opportunity to apply for a United States Permanent Resident Card.

There was no guarantee. The article explained how to enter for a chance to win an interview with an American consular officer. The odds of winning sounded worse than a bad gambling game. But an athlete who doesn't suit up, will never be a player. A person who doesn't buy a ticket, will never win the draw, so I mailed my name to the address indicated, not knowing if the contest was even still active or was a hoax. I told my family and my girlfriend, and their reactions were dispassionate. I'm sure they thought the obvious: *Not likely.*

———

The air turned cold, and the Bârlad River near home iced over as we braced for winter weather. My American dream soon chilled as well and faded from focus.

The calendar clung to November 1993.

———

During the six months that followed until the spring flowers of May were in full bloom, I focused on my true love, the woman with whom

I wanted to spend the rest of my life. Her birth name was Gabriela. I had not yet proposed to her, but I knew without question that she was my life love.

In May 1994, a large, official-looking envelope arrived at my parents' home. My brother and I had overlapping off-duty hours, and we were home working on his car. The envelope was delivered by a mailman on bicycle with a leather mailbag slung across his shoulders. He liked to stop and bring our mail to the door, as Dad often would invite him in and offer a glass of house wine.

"Something for you, Nicolae," the mailman shouted to me as he dismounted his bicycle and walked to the front door of our home.

I looked quizzically at Marin, but he simply reached for another tool. We did not get junk mail. That plague had not yet spread across Romania. Official documents in large envelopes had always been for Dad from the court system, usually bearing bad news, but this one was addressed to me.

I finished the task with Marin and then headed toward the house, wiping my hands on a cloth rag as I walked. I tucked the rag in my pants pocket and combed my fingers through my hair.

The mailman was finishing his glass of wine as I entered the kitchen door. He tipped his hat to bid me good day, thanked my father for the warmth of wine, and left.

Dad extended the large envelope to me, and I inspected the official markings. Mom fidgeted at the cupboard. I carefully sliced open one end of the envelope and pulled out the documents. I could not read the contents written in English, but I knew immediately that this was real, the answer to my dream.

I looked up into the eyes of Mom. I was her youngest son. She wanted the best for me, but she had hoped I would not win this lottery.

Her eyes moistened with the clarity of reflective glass and then a tear escaped and rolled down her weathered cheek.

Dad did not show emotions, and I understood this was the defense mechanism he used to survive.

"I'll need to find someone to read it," I said, breaking the silence. "I'll ask Marin to drive me to Galați."

I sensed a head nod from both parents, and I turned and stepped out the door.

Marin and I finished fixing the car and took off toward Galați to find a friend who knew English and could read the letter. I did not have a way to call him ahead of time, but I had confidence we would locate him. My friend knew I had applied for what I called the "liberty lottery," and like me, he doubted it would happen. We found him at the second stop in Galați, after making one inquiry.

"There is urgency in your eyes," he said as I bolted from the car with a smile locked on my face.

His eyes darted to the envelope I waved like a flag of freedom.

"What is it?" he asked, but he knew without my answer.

With the warm wind blowing my hair I inhaled the smell of springtime while I waited for my friend to read the envelope contents carefully.

As he translated, the gravity of the offer began sinking in. I looked at my brother for support. He was always giving me money, so maybe he would be happy I was going to be on my own. I could read his feelings like a book without a cover. We had grown closer after our military service years, and he seemed to respect me more as a peer and a friend.

The document said not to quit my job, nor assume that the offer was final acceptance or a done deal. It simply said I had won the opportunity to be interviewed. There were about 4,800 openings allocated to Romanian citizens. The odds were stacked against me, but I had already beaten the odds by winning this first round.

"I'm stunned—and excited!" I beamed.

I wanted to tell everyone. *What was possibly more important to talk about?* But the next morning I started my twenty-four-hour work shift, so my contact with others was limited to the riverboat crew.

My riverboat captain grinned from ear to ear and gave me a bear hug instead of a professional handshake when I told him the news. There were no cell phones, so I had no way to contact Gabriela. I wanted to tell her in person anyway.

When my shift ended, I took the bus to the city of Brăila, hoping to find Gabriela at her apartment, but she was not there. I didn't care if the sun set on my search; I had to find her. She had taken a five-minute walk to her girlfriend's apartment, and that was the next place I looked.

Gabriela had no way of knowing I was coming, so she was surprised to see me. I had the envelope hidden from her view, but her first words were, "Why are you so happy? Don't tell me—you are going to America!"

I pulled out the envelope and held it toward her.

"Yes!" I said.

"We are going to America!"

Gabriela jumped into my arms and hugged my neck so hard I thought she might choke me.

———

Over the next week, I prepared paperwork as the letter instructed, trying to be proactive, but it then took two months to get an appointment at the American embassy. The process required an initial interview, which I thought went well, but the embassy emphasized that I did not have final approval. There were still many hurdles to jump, from medical exams to criminal background checks, which dragged on the remainder of the year.

———

In February 1995, I was invited back to the American embassy, and Gabriela went with me, but she was allowed only as far as the waiting room. I was escorted to a private room, handed a visa, and told to be ready in six months to start life anew in America. Somehow, I did not feel prepared for the moment. Maybe it was because Gabriela was not beside me.

"My fiancée is sitting in the waiting room. I need to secure a visa for her as well," I said.

"You are not married." The customs officer raised an eyebrow.

"We are getting married, and we will be going together."

"Your wife can apply for a visa after your marriage and meet up with you in America later," he reassured.

"How long will that take?" I asked.

I noticed a faint furrow in the officer's forehead. He seemed to be choosing his words carefully. "Not long, Nicolae. It is the process ... the right process. You should feel proud that you have this opportunity to start your life in America. You can get settled, and then we can work on getting her visa secured."

"How long is 'not long'?" I stared into his eyes without blinking.

He blinked—more than once.

"Three years," he replied, biting the edge of his lower lip.

I laid my visa back down on the table, slid it toward him, and said, "I won't go without her!"

My words echoed off the four walls, slicing the silence. The official did not speak for several moments, his eyes darting from mine to my visa lying on the table. I had made up my mind. *They can either refuse one or accept two. Gabriela and I are going together or not at all.*

The official finally broke the silence and again tried to convince me otherwise. When I refused to retract my decision, he summoned an associate to bring Gabriela from the waiting room. I turned to gaze out the window, expressing my disinterest in negotiating with him. There were few trees planted in the sterile courtyard, so my view was unobstructed. White cumulous clouds drifted in the summer blue sky.

Gabriela's approaching footsteps drew my thoughts back into the moment, and I was already smiling when she graced the door opening. I arose to welcome her to my side and pulled out the chair for her to join us at the table. Our fingers locked, and we leaned into each other as we sat down. The consular officer started to rise but flushed when he realized it was too late, so he leaned across the table and extended his hand as he said hello.

There wasn't any need for small talk.

"Do you have your wedding date set?" He directed the question to Gabriela.

"The third of June," she responded.

He told us to come back after the wedding, but he stressed that this exception was not normal.

Gabriela squeezed my hand so tightly that I winced. The "exception" meant my request had been accepted. This would be a wedding present and honeymoon unlike any we had envisioned.

A ticket to freedom and a new lifestyle came without instructions or a teacher. There was no government handout or any free lunch. America was known to be the promised land of opportunity and freedom, but Gabriela and I agreed it would be best for me to confirm it before we both planted our lives there. The American government required that I have a place to go and someone to live with, a sponsor, who could introduce me to this new lifestyle upon arrival in the United States.

The only person I knew who might be living in America was Constantin, the neighbor kid who had defected several years earlier. Rumor was that he had survived.

45

Winds of Change

~ Spring 1995 ~

IT was meant to be. There was a reason for it all and how it all turned out. I see it even more clearly now than I did at the time.

———

"Good morning, Nicolae. I heard the good news. Are you excited?"

I was visiting with Constantin's mother, standing on her front porch. Our families knew each other well, and I felt comfortable with the question I came to ask. Constantin's father was not home from work, but I felt confident his parents were in unison.

"It still feels like a dream, but a dream that's coming true," I replied. "In fact, that is why I stopped by today, because, to make it a reality, I need to ask your permission and a huge favor from Constantin."

Her smile was warm and her eyes bright.

"I need a sponsor—someone I can stay with when I land on American soil. I wondered if Constantin would serve in that role."

She rushed forward and embraced me as she would her own son. She sobbed as I hugged her and then whispered, "Finally ... our son will not be alone."

———

When Constantin had all but given up his river escape, his body settling upright and his arms thrusting in one last attempt to keep his head above water, his feet had touched river bottom. He had crawled ashore and lain on his back, gasping and staring into the nighttime sky. Had he made it to Yugoslavia or ended up back in Romania?

Constantin was one of the lucky defectors. His head was resting on Yugoslavian soil. He had made it.

––––––

Constantin was not actually alone; he had married a Japanese woman, and they had a newborn boy. I knew what his mother meant. She was overjoyed to know her son would have a fellow Romanian to connect with—to share stories about Torceşti and all the good and not so good times we both had experienced in the past eight years.

St. Louis, Missouri, sounded so foreign and faraway. But it was home to her son, and now her grandson, who had never met his Romanian grandma.

One more connection. One more opportunity. I could take her love and hand-deliver it to her son and his little family. I contacted Constantin, and he was elated. He was honored to be my sponsor and welcoming party.

––––––

On July 12, 1995, I boarded a flight to St. Louis via Atlanta. I did not consider it "goodbye"—my last words to Gabriela had been, "I will see you soon."

This was my first flight, ever. The roar of the jet engines and the thrust of take-off could not keep me from leaning forward and pressing my nose against the window. The plane rose, and the earth fell away beneath me. I had never experienced the sensation of rising above the earth.

I thought of Constantin and how similar my thoughts might be to his when he had pushed off from the Romanian shore and floated by faith toward the promise of a better future. But his journey had been much more dangerous. Leaving home and moving to a different part of the country is nothing like leaving one's homeland.

I was not running *from* anything, but *to* something. I had a dream, an aspiration for life filled with adventure, freedom, and opportunity. I could hear the whinny of Simi and the whisper of my parents and grandpa to hold my head high and live free.

The Romanian countryside looked breathtaking from the air. The expanse of terrain filled my view to a panoramic proportion faster than I could grasp the details as we climbed to cruising altitude. I was amazed the territorial lines that divided nations were not visible.

I strained to catch the last glimpse of Romania on the horizon, and then I looked west to the arc of the landscape ahead. The air at this height was thin, but the future seemed thick with endless possibilities.

The winds of change were in motion as I settled back in my seat and closed my eyes.

Epilogue

~ Summer 2005 ~

THE wind changes direction, bringing my mind back to the present. I stand in the middle of this long-ago tomato field flooded with memories. When news of my father's death had arrived in 2004, I was in America and could not attend the funeral. I came to pay tribute to my father's legacy and now am reluctant to leave.

My father was destined to be a liberator at heart: inspiring hope, defending freedoms, and resisting the oppression of tyranny. It was in his DNA, the fiber from which he was woven. He did not become a partisan or one of the anti-communist resistance fighters who willingly participated in military operations in hopes of overthrowing communism. He was a gentle man, driven by an inner strength that influenced every aspect of my life.

Morning sunlight penetrates the stillness, ripening my senses. Mist dances from the soil, floating upward with memories of the past dissolving into the warmth of a new day. The field is a deep-rooted symbol of our family's struggle for freedom and independence—our struggle for life.

These experiences shaped a nation, and these experiences shaped a young boy. I learned lessons no textbook could ever teach. Life has been good, and life has been hard, but there are no regrets.

My father would be proud to see all I have done, where I have traveled, and the liberty and stability I have in my life.

I close my eyes. I can feel his presence.

My father was an inspiration, a winner.

He was Ionel (Cuța) Cismigiu—The Tomato Farmer.

Like father, like son.

Grandpa Neculai with his two sisters (prior to his death in 1971)

Cuţa before he was married

MARK LEE MYERS

Antonia before she was married

Cuţa, Antonia, Marin, Lenuţa (c. 1969)

Antonia & Cuţa (c. 1981)

En route to county fair – Cuţa holding horse reins (c. 1960)

Transplanting. Kneeling on boards to prevent damaging plants

Cuța & Nicolae transplanting tomato plants

Cuța, Nicolae & Lenuța weeding tomato plants in greenhouses

Greenhouse full of transplanted tomato plants

*Nicolae, Lenuța, Cuța, Antonia inspecting greenhouse
tomato plants*

Cuța planting tomatoes

Cuţa planting (c. 1986)

Portion of planted tomato field with support poles ready for installation

Communist officials overseeing the destruction of springtime planting

Portion of tomato field planted and prepared with irrigation troughs

Cuţa arguing with police come to destroy tomato plants (c. 1983)

MARK LEE MYERS

Communist official in the act of destroying newly planted crop

*Cuța pointing to remains after Communists
destroyed family vineyard*

*Cuța documenting evidence of his family's vineyard
destroyed by Communists*

About the Author

Mark and his wife, Jeanette, were childhood sweethearts and have shared a great life together.

Mark is a Storyteller. He speaks with passion and writes with a natural voice to give others the gift he gives to himself: a deepened curiosity and broadened perspective.

Mark loves the realism of life stories—to preserve and share them. He is an explorer at heart who immensely enjoys meeting people and learning their love of life, song of spirit, and struggles of endurance—the things that make them uniquely different and yet so similar.

I'm at home with a poor man,
At ease with a king,
And I fit right in with all those in-between.

—Mark Lee Myers, 1981

CPSIA information can be obtained
at www.ICGtesting.com
Printed in the USA
FSHW011852030521
81092FS